Books by Yuri Brokhin

Hustling on Gorky Street
The Big Red Machine: The Rise and Fall
of Soviet Sports Champions

THE
BIG RED
MACHINE

Random House
New York

[c 1978]

THE
BIG RED
MACHINE

○━○━━━━━○━○

The Rise and Fall of
Soviet Olympic Champions

○━○━━━━━○━○

Yuri Brokhin

Translated from the Russian by
Glenn Garelik and Yuri Brokhin

Library of Congress Cataloging in Publication Data
Brokhin, Yuri, 1934-
The big red machine.
1. Sports and state—Russia. 2. Olympic games.
3. Sports—Philosophy. 4. Athletes—Russia—
Biography. I. Title.
GV623.B76   796′.0947   77-90284
ISBN 0-394-41078-5

A portion of this book previously appeared in
The New York Times Magazine.
Manufactured in the United States of America
2 4 6 8 9 7 5 3
First Edition

CONTENTS

THE
BIG RED
MACHINE

ONE

How to Kill an Athlete

Colonel Vladimir Kuts, an outstanding athlete who brought honor to Soviet sports at stadiums the world over, died today after a long and serious illness.

—Tass, August 16, 1975

In 1954 Vladimir Kuts set his first world record in the 5,000 meters with a time of 13:56:6, beating Emil Zatopek, the Czech champion of the Helsinki Olympics.

Kuts liked to set a fast pace, taking the front of the pack immediately and holding it from gun to tape. But in the 5,000 meters in a 1955 meet between London and Moscow, Christopher Chataway stayed on Kuts's shoulder all the way and outkicked him in the final meter.

In the spring of 1956 another English runner, Gordon Pirie, beat Kuts in the 10,000 meters with an identical kick from just behind and broke the world record. After the race, Pirie invited the crowd over the loudspeaker to applaud Kuts for setting him up for the victory.

The media hubbub over the Russian's rivalry with the two Englishmen reached its peak toward the end of 1956 during the Melbourne Olympics. While track experts gave the odds to Pirie and Chataway, they all had to admit that Kuts was someone to be reckoned with.

Melbourne Stadium was jammed to a capacity 70,000. The spectators might have been carrying neutral program notes but, hyped on the newspaper and TV controversy, no one could remain uninvolved. Betting was rampant.

In the 10,000 meters Kuts burst from the starting line like a sprinter, but Pirie matched him immediately. Five laps into the race Kuts suddenly upped the pace and left Pirie 15 meters behind. Pirie caught up. Kuts pulled five more spurts in a row. In the eighth lap he slowed up abruptly and the Englishman slammed into him. Almost stopping, Kuts waved his hand as if suggesting that Pirie take the lead. The Englishman declined the courtesy. In the meantime the main pack was approaching and threatening to leave the two gentlemen negotiating in the dust. Kuts started jogging, and the crowd thought he was ready to drop off. The fact was that Kuts was playing out a strategy, breaking Pirie down with his spurts and confusing him by laying back from his usual lead.

The other runners—Kenneth Norris of England, Allan Lawrence of Australia, Herbert Schade of West Germany, Jozsef Kovacs of Hungary—would have swallowed them up in another second when Kuts suddenly spurted powerfully, as though boosted by the latest Siberian power station. In the lead until the twentieth lap, Kuts looked straight ahead but listened carefully to Pirie's breathing behind him. As if his ears were outfitted with radar, he computed the distance between them. At maximum speed on the straightaway, when Kuts knew that Pirie was less than a meter behind, he shifted unexpectedly to the inside and slowed up sharply. Pirie raced past and, against his will, took over the lead. From behind, Kuts could examine his opponent. He saw that Pirie was worn out. He looked shorter, weighted down by fatigue. Kuts moved onto Pirie's right shoulder and prepared for the finish kick. This time his own breathing let the Englishman know that he was nearby and still in control of the race. Kuts began his kick with two laps to go and left Pirie far behind, seven more runners passing him by the time it was over. Kuts had finished in the record time of 28:30:4.

"He murdered me," Pirie admitted. "I couldn't take that switching the pace. It was torture."

The next day Kuts beat Chataway in the 5,000 meters, completely settling accounts with the Englishmen and winning the Soviet Union its first gold medal for track and field in Olympic history. The Soviet coaches, teammates, and sports directors showered him with congratulations.

An hour after the awards ceremony, Kuts was taken for a medical examination. Years later the Soviet physician admitted he had been stunned to see the blue lips, pale face, panting, and feverish pulse of a man in the middle of a race—long after the run had ended.

A digression on physiology and pre-Melbourne matters: running consumes energy liberated upon the oxidation of glucose in the muscles. This glucose is regularly replenished by eating, but even if a person goes for a considerable time without food, the body retains a glucose reserve.

With oxygen, there is no such reserve. The oxygen used in the burning of glucose is supplied to the blood moment to moment, picked up in the lungs and sent to the heart, which in turn pumps it to all parts of the body—legs, arms, head. The more oxygen entering the bloodstream, the brighter the blaze of the glucose in the muscles, the more energy liberated, and the faster the speed of the runner. During a race the average man uses up three liters of oxygen a minute. A trained long-distance runner, on the other hand, can consume five or six liters. Vladimir Kuts could handle seven, and another Russian long-distance runner, Pëtr Bolotnikov, 5,000-meter gold medalist at the Rome Olympics, averaged 7.3. But neither of them, nor any other long-distance runner, has been able to make use of all of the oxygen the lungs take in. From a physiological point of view, the training of a long-distance runner is a process of learning to extract as much oxygen as possible from the very bottom of the lungs, where it tends to settle. If a person is ever found who is capable of emptying his lungs completely, he will automatically set new world records—even with a heart of less than superior natural strength.

The condition of an athlete's heart is measured by the number of beats per minute: the less the better. Kuts had a pulse of 45 at rest and 120 racing. (Others have as low as 35 and 100, respectively.) Heart size is also important. The volume of the heart in the average nonrunner is 750–780 cubic centimeters; Kuts's was 1,026.

There is as yet no consensus among the world's physicians and scientists as to the causes of cardiac enlargement in athletes (a phenomenon that appears particularly in skiers, runners, cyclists, and rowers). Some physicians begin from the logical assumption that only a massive organ can pump the large amounts of oxygenated blood needed by the athlete. They consider this "work hypertrophy" normal—a thickening of the cardiac muscle, like any other muscle in the body, in response to intensified workloads.

According to Professor Aleksandr Gendelsman, who did regular checkups of Kuts, in mid-1956 all of the athlete's physiological indicators were satisfactory, if not up to those of the other Russian long-distance runners. But by that time it had also become clear that the fast, even-paced strategy that had captured the 5,000-meter world record for Kuts in 1954 had failed against the Englishmen and would no longer work.

In the four months that remained before the Olympics, Coach Grigorii Nikiforov decided to try a new strategy and drastically restructured his whole training system. And, at a meeting of the party cell of the Soviet Olympic team, Kuts and Nikiforov agreed to sign a "socialist pledge" to win medals for the motherland at Melbourne Stadium —a written promise to achieve winning results.

The slogan ALL WORLD RECORDS MUST BE TAKEN BY SOVIET ATHLETES—above a mammoth picture of a virile young man and a rosy-cheeked girl beaming happily under the hammer and sickle—towered over stadiums across the Soviet Union in the 1950s. Youngsters went around singing a tune that began, "Anyone can become a hero when the motherland demands it!"

The passage of time has tempered the state's appeals. Russian athletes are now exhorted just to "mount an attack on world records," as though Soviet leaders are finally willing to allow that others might occasionally take a share in the glory.

These "attacks" are often timed to coincide with the nation's great jubilees: the centenary of Lenin's birth, the fiftieth anniversary of the Bolshevik Revolution, the twenty-fifth anniversary of the victory over Nazi Germany. In between these major occasions, celebrations of medium caliber are available, like Steelworkers' Day, Teachers' Day, or Fishermen's Day, and minifestivals, such as the tenth anniversary of a provincial cement factory. The party's powerful press and propaganda apparatus are launched at the entire populace in the period preceding these occasions.

Workers are also obliged to take "elevated" socialist pledges to produce two times more coal, steel, oil, or bicycles. Engineers promise to design new machines. Railroad workers swear to speed up the trains. Hospital personnel, on the same principle—the more the better—declare their readiness to process 100 percent more patients, dead or alive. Music teachers rack their brains to cultivate a couple of Oistrakhs and half a dozen new Gilelses apiece.

The jubilees keep the people busy and serve as psychological shots in the arm to the athletes. Weight lifter Vasilii Alekseev has attributed fully half of his eighty world records to various political events. But if the Twenty-fourth Congress of the Communist Party was worthy of breaking his old record by a whole 10 kilograms, Athletes' Day warranted only 2—leaving a solid reserve for the next extravaganza.

The Olympics, of course, eclipse all internal political gimmickry. With the approach of the Games, athletes begin a period of intensified training. Coaches, physicians, and scientists join forces to squeeze the maximum results —whether meters, kilograms, or seconds—from the athletes in the minimum time.

The athletes participate in these experiments willingly,

though never sure what the consequences of sudden, huge overloads will be on their health.

In August of 1956, Kuts, who had been putting in over 40 kilometers a day, began to cover the same distance broken up into shorter segments. He would do five lengths at 2,000 meters each and ten at 1,000, all faster than long-distance speed, and finish with ten 600-meter dashes and thirty at 400 meters. Coach Nikiforov was fully convinced that his "variational" workout, in combination with an athlete the likes of Kuts, had given him a sure-fire record breaker.

To justify the system scientifically, Nikiforov developed a theory according to which the athlete's body should be capable of bearing any overload if artfully manipulated by diet, massage, sleep, training schedule, and proper psychological environment. Early every morning Nikiforov made Kuts a bowl of oatmeal in which every grain was scrupulously strained for impurities. At lunch he would feed him boiled chicken. He supplemented this according to elaborate schemes with proteins, carbohydrates, and vitamins C and A. He argued violently with the team cooks if he discovered Kuts's steak had been overdone.

Kuts was turned into something that no longer ate but simply carried out the physiological process of ingestion; that no longer slept but took part in a slowdown of cardiovascular activity; that no longer made love but read articles airmailed by his wife Raisa, a correspondent for *Sovetskii Sport*.

After two months and 1,600 miles of workouts on a track, Kuts was transferred out of the stadium to ten 2,000-meter heats in heavy army boots with a sandbag on his back. In the afternoons, Nikiforov would collect twenty-five athletes to run 10,000-meter relays against Kuts alone, alternating the speed of each leg from 68 seconds to 60 and back.

Kuts later said in an interview with a Soviet journalist that "Nikiforov seemed like an executioner—determined to break me down, body and soul. What he was actually doing was solidly programmed to make a warrior of me, capable of enduring any stresses of sports combat. . . ."

Kuts said nothing (being well tutored for Soviet-style showcase interviews) about the condition of his heart, which Nikiforov's homemade theory had failed to keep healthy. By the fourth month of training his heart had grown another 45 cubic centimeters, making for a total volume of 1,071.

X-rays indicated acute lateral expansion of both right and left ventricles: a heart with work hypertrophy had been turned into a dangerously distended balloon, barely contained by his mere 5'7", 159-pound body.

Two weeks before the Olympics, Kuts showed symptoms that Nikiforov diagnosed as a combination of overtraining and precontest nerves. His resting pulse was 120; his blood pressure, 180/105. Heart murmurs were detected. The athlete seemed occasionally listless and virtually indifferent to running. If he managed his daily mileage at all, his motor continued racing for the next forty-eight hours.

The training was called off, and Kuts went to Melbourne not knowing whether he would make it to the starting line. While most of the team inaugurated a new TU-104 turbo-prop to Delhi and DC-8s through Rangoon and Singapore to Australia, Kuts sailed there on the ocean liner *Gruziia*. For sixteen days he took in the sea air, eating borsch, shashlik, and kasha—and occasionally, to Nikiforov's horror, sipping a bit of cognac.

In Melbourne, the runner went through more than a dozen workouts in the presence of coaches from all over the world, who conscientiously filmed his sprints. His ocean voyage seemed to have restored in him the constancy of performance of a robot.

Soviet physicians found Kuts's heart entirely normal, with the exception of its size (the limits of enlargement are still unknown, twenty years later), and chalked up the previous irregularities as something that could happen to any athlete.

It was only his state of semicollapse after the 5,000 meters that made Kuts realize he was in trouble. Nevertheless, after a two-month break, he returned to training.

"We could all see that he was only a shadow of himself," said his teammate Bolotnikov. "He had become unrecognizable. Nikiforov would order, say, an hour of paced running, and Kuts could barely make it. He would order five sets of two thousand meters and Kuts would come in last. Anyone could beat him. He lost to everyone, absolutely everyone . . . But we couldn't bring ourselves to ask what was wrong. He was really kind of hard to talk to."

Still, in September of 1957, Kuts broke through what seemed to be his physical limits at an international meet in Rome with a 13:35:0 5,000 meters—a time surpassed only eight years later by the Australian Ron Clarke.

Fifteen years later Bolotnikov, who at the time had lost to Kuts, said, "Here I was—healthy, but a loser. I was ashamed of myself when they carried the great runner off the track on a stretcher after the heat. . . ." Kuts was taken directly from the stadium to the hospital. At the age of twenty-nine, when most long-distance runners are entering their peak, the doctors informed the Olympic champion that he could never run again.

In the years following World War II, most long-distance runners were trained in the German "interval" system. The athlete who could cover the greatest total distance during training was considered to have the advantage in the real thing. In many ways it was Zatopek who initiated Nikiforov's "variational" system, a model for actual competitions by accelerating the speed in sections so that the athlete would feel at home on the day of the event.

Nikiforov's system, which also accented diet and regime, turned out to be disastrous. Kuts became a bundle of nerves in reaction to the discomfort. His dietary negligence on the *Gruziia*, on the other hand, served to relax him.

Nikiforov's really important discovery was the cat-and-mouse strategy and the technique of momentary periods of relaxation during long-distance races. Kuts, as the Africans later demonstrated quite spectacularly, taught himself to relax toward the end of every spurt, rolling with the momentum of the previous pace and, in the pause, refreshing himself for the next burst of speed.

Australia's Percy Cerutti and Arthur Lydiard of New Zealand acknowledged the impact of Nikiforov and Kuts on their own methods in training Herb Elliott, Peter Snell, Murray Halberg, and Ron Clarke, who ran the varied sections even faster than Kuts. Elliott, an Olympic champion and the best student of the over-the-hill-and-into-the-valley school, took up heavy weight lifting and the torture of sprinting through surf and sand.

Like other long-distance runners of the new generation,

Elliott had begun running at around the age of seven, when natural running technique seems to match that of the champions. As they grow older and become less active, children lose this talent. But those who are grabbed up by a good trainer can develop stamina by the age of ten (at ten, Elliott was doing a 6:50 mile, and at fourteen, a 5:35). With fifteen or twenty years of gradually increasing workloads—and without official pledges to break world records overnight—the athletes of Australia and New Zealand emerged as the greatest long-distance runners of the sixties.

Before the age of twenty-one, Kuts had no idea he would go into sports. While serving as a marine in Tallinn, he had to pass the regular physical fitness course and choose a sport to specialize in. He took up boxing. After a year of training he had won several provincial matches but found himself less interested. It's possible that he would have remained an aspiring boxer if his unit hadn't been transferred to Leningrad.

In Leningrad he met Nikiforov and, at twenty-three, found himself on a track for the first time in his life. His body—lean, narrow-shouldered, slightly stooped—was a far cry from the classic image of the athlete. Great victories in sports come from something unseen: a capacity to withstand torture. Kuts was a Russian peasant—a unique branch of mankind that has survived silently through four centuries of Mongol hordes, three centuries of czars, and sixty years of Soviet Communism.

Russians have remained mute while being strung up on the gallows, when hot lead was being poured down their throats, upon finding their huts destroyed or their children dead from hunger, when burning up in the holds of ships or freezing to death in labor camps. This silence has penetrated their genes; it has become part of their hereditary code, and anger, pain, bitterness, and resentment remain sealed in their hearts until they explode in infarction.

Kuts had been transplanted by a quirk of fate from rural pastures to big-city stadiums, but he remained a Russian peasant, running, with lips tight and barely parted, the muscles of his face unmoving, against runners grimacing with pain. Arthur Daley, an American sports writer who saw him at Melbourne, wrote in *The Story of the Olympic Games* that "his remorselessness was frightening. . . . If Kuts has to kill himself to kill off the opposition, he has enough suicidal dedication to run himself to death."

When Kuts's heart began sending warning signals, he responded like a Russian marine instructed not to retreat from his position until ordered to do so. Finally retired by the doctors, he had to begin the long, slow process of unloading the 45,000 miles accumulated in his seven years as a runner. The only remedy was to run again every day for three or four years, slowly decreasing the pace and mileage. But that was no longer possible. Instead, he was transferred from hospital to hospital, his EKG and X-rays failing to improve.

Kuts's heart continued to pump huge amounts of blood into inactive arms and legs, which no longer needed it and resisted the oversupply, pushing the blood back and creating new disorders.

In 1960 Kuts had his first heart attack. The government gave him a pension and a petty bureaucratic position at the Central Army Club, but he rarely showed up. Occasionally he would come to an international meet at the stadium. His bloated face, with dark bags under the eyes, would quickly become covered with perspiration. He'd take out a handkerchief, wipe his face, and take a breath, opening his mouth wide, as though yawning. The spectators would point to him. He would turn red and sweaty again, again wipe his face, slowly lift his 230 pounds and walk away. Photographers chased after him but never received permission to print their shots. Kuts died in his sleep from his fourth heart attack.

In 1970, at the age of twenty-one, the gymnast Natasha Kuchinskaia, Olympic champion at Mexico, was retired from sports. Six months later she found herself in a hospital with cardiac arrest. Only then was it discovered that she was suffering from thyrotoxicosis, a dysfunction that had thrown her entire hormonal system off balance. Within a year her body bulged from 98 pounds to 170. She would come into the gym and, with tears in her eyes, beg to be pulled up onto the bars.

It was gymnastics, as physical culture, that had made Natasha a slender and beautiful girl at seventeen. It was gymnastics, too, as merciless competition, that had ruined her at twenty-four. Natasha's case, though never publicized by the Soviet media, became a subject of concern and debate among coaches, who had begun to wonder just what it was they were really doing.

In 1972 Viktor Lonskii, widely respected in track and field and an Honored Coach of the Soviet Union, dared to write: "Our athletes are dying young. I can mention facts, staggering facts; I can name names, cheered not so long ago in stadiums throughout the world. But the important thing isn't the names or any cheap sensationalism. What's important is that a well-known weight lifter becomes a serious heart case as a young man, a famous runner is in need of constant treatment, an outstanding gymnast is dying at thirty-three, and a renowned boxer has become an invalid. You won't find anything about them in the press. But can their fate not help but force us to rethink our slogan 'Sport Is Health'?"

In this small book, *What Can Be Said about the Heights,* a Soviet publishing anomaly that sold out instantly, Lonskii wrote: "It's shocking how little interested we are in anything unconnected with breaking records. We direct the science of sports exclusively at putting our athletes in peak condition, but does anyone concern himself with what happens when an intensively trained individual has to switch over to a more moderate regimen? Does anyone worry when a top athlete retires from sports, 'going nowhere,' quite literally?"

It is possible that in the distant future Soviet science will discover an athlete's precise limits of endurance, that it will develop an electronic meter for which a fatal load will cause a light to flash and an oscilloscope that will signal the breakdown zones with a desperate buzz.

But new Kuchinskaias and new Kutses, equipped with detailed schedules of the tragedies to come, will march toward them anyway. Neither the political system nor its commissars will have to put a gun to their heads; they will only have to offer to sign a socialist pledge. A tradition.

TWO

In Search of Challenge

The July 23, 1962, issue of *The New York Times* pictured high jumper Valerii Brumel clearing a world-record 7' 5" at Stanford University Stadium. The article below the photo proclaimed the Soviet-American meet "the greatest track-and-field spectacle California has seen since the '32 Olympics."

The early sixties saw Brumel's name emerge as a household word. In three years he toppled the world mark six times—in a sport in which it usually took a decade to raise it half an inch.

Brumel was named UPI athlete of the year in 1961, 1962, and 1963. Nikita Khrushchev invited him to the Kremlin and John Kennedy received him at the White House. At twenty-two he walked off with Olympic gold.

Tall and well-built, the black-haired Brumel had the face of an artist inspired by some secret acquaintance with man's innermost potential. When he married one of the most beautiful women in Moscow, a photo of the pair appeared on magazine covers throughout the Socialist world.

On October 4, 1965, having predictably made short work of the annual French-Russian duel, Brumel flew home from Paris and was back training as a track-and-field student at Moscow's Institute of Physical Culture without losing a day. Since his wife had gone shopping in their new Mercedes, he asked Tamara Golikova, a good friend and a Master of Sport in motorcycle racing, for a lift home after practice.

"I sat behind Tamara on the cycle," Brumel relates, "concocting strategies. Everything was going well for me, and Moscow seemed never to have looked better. The wet streets all over the fresh, cheery city glistened with the recent rain. Doing eighty along Iauzskaia Embankment, we splashed through a puddle and plunged into the dark underpass at Dvortsovyi Bridge. Once out of the underpass, we started to turn off when the bike skidded and went crashing into the stone ramp along the shoulder. I went flying out of the saddle and hit a concrete pillar. Everything went black. As I came to, I tried to move my arms; they were O.K. I touched my head; it was all right, too. My take-off leg seemed fine. Then I glanced at my other leg. A stark white piece of bone was sticking out from under the knee. And my foot? All I saw was an empty shoe lying fifteen feet away. Suddenly, behind me, I heard a truck barreling out of the tunnel start to gnash and screech. Under its headlights, for the first time, I noticed the blood alongside me and the chips of bone. I realized my foot was under me, hanging by no more than a few tendons.

"Now Tamara came running. She had missed the piling

and escaped without a scratch. As she flagged down a cab, I literally picked up the foot in my left hand and hopped over to the taxi on the other leg."

The best surgeons in Moscow were called into Sklifosovskii Hospital. Several were concerned about gangrene and wanted to amputate. The doctor in charge opted for surgical repair, but he told Brumel the obvious: he was through as an athlete. The best he could hope for was a limp and a cane for the rest of his life.

One of the numerous telegrams rushed to the hospital after the accident came from Boston: SOMETIMES A TWIST OF FATE SEEMS TO HAVE BEEN PUT THERE TO TEST A MAN'S STRENGTH OF CHARACTER. DON'T ADMIT DEFEAT. I SINCERELY HOPE YOU COME BACK TO JUMP AGAIN. JOHN THOMAS.

Seven years before, while a high school student in the industrial city of Voroshilovgrad, Brumel had read a notice in *Sovetskii Sport* about the amazing sixteen-year-old Thomas, who had just cleared 6′ 7½″. Brumel was fifteen and doing only 5′ 8¾″.

Brumel was the kind of boy who had to be tops in everything, whether math or schoolyard fights. He hurled a silent challenge at the American.

As it turned out, Pëtr Shein, Brumel's high school coach, knew next to nothing about high jumping. But he *was* big on weight lifting. . . .

Popular opinion had it that weight lifting wouldn't strengthen a jumper's legs but only get in the way during the approach run. Shein was convinced of the opposite: weight lifting would build take-off power. He saw the jumper's body as a missile that could be launched only if the lead leg could push off with at least 500 kilograms.

Brumel worked up to a 110-kilogram snatch-from-a-squat and an 85-kilogram clean-and-jerk. Within a year his long legs were rippling with powerful muscles.

Once he cleared 6' 6¾", Brumel felt ready to place a trans-Atlantic call to Thomas on the growing Russian threat. But by that time Thomas had bested 7'.

While scouting, Coach Vladimir Diachkov had noticed Brumel's unusual determination, and at seventeen the jumper was picked up by the USSR National Team. The offer came as a surprise to the boy himself, who was living in a Lvov dormitory with 12 drunken roommates, earning a hundred rubles a month at a fat- and oil-processing combine, and spending every kopeck of it on high-energy foods for training after an exhausting day's work.

Catapulted to Moscow, the luxury of a 250-ruble stipend and a two-man-per-room training camp, Brumel seized his good break like a ravenous lion.

"When we first began working together," said Diachkov, "he asked me more questions than I had heard in all my years as a trainer put together."

The mysteries of the straddle roll were laid bare to Brumel day after day. He clocked a 10.8-second 100 meters. He shook off his nagging prejump tension and got down a heel-to-toe run, leaning into the bar just two steps before pushing off. It wasn't long before he was in shape for the main feature of his coach's course: sailing over the bar at nearly the speed of the run-up, using his lead foot the way a vaulter does his pole.

To translate horizontal speed into vertical with minimal waste, an athlete has to combine a kangaroo's kicking power with the coordination of a squirrel. Brumel plumbed the deep secrets of animal gymnastics and blended them with human determination. After eight months he had worked himself up to 7' 1½".

In the meantime the Soviet media weren't offering any news about Thomas, and a hunger for information led Brumel to Moscow's main library. Knowing that American papers and magazines were guarded in a special reading room by pistol-packing plainclothesmen, the inquisitive star-to-be counterarmed himself with written Sports Committee permission. Brumel hunted through stacks of the *Times* for three days and nights before stumbling upon the following headline: "Thomas Catches Foot in Elevator Shaft." With his meager high school English, he wondered what sort of man his American rival must be to catch someone's foot in the bone-crushing mechanism. Librarians helped clarify the issue.

Whether or not the injury would affect Thomas's performance, simple arithmetic told the eighteen-year-old Brumel that he had made it over the top with his latest jump of 7' 1½": the American had hit half an inch less at the same age.

But Brumel's triumphant mood didn't last long. On April 30, 1960, *Sovetskii Sport* reported that Thomas had cleared 7' 1½" in Philadelphia. And before the type could dry in the latest sports books he showered them with new results: on May 21, 7' 1¾"; on June 24, 7' 2"; on June 29, 7' 3¾"—a new world record.

Brumel's silent call to arms finally brought him face-to-face with Thomas in Rome, where he and two friends watched as the American trained in Aquacitoza Stadium. Thomas's body radiated enormous strength. With a smirk he walked up to the soccer goal, planted his right leg on the ground, and lifted his left foot easily to the crossbar.

When a companion whispered that the Russians were observing, Thomas grinned again, set the high-jump bar at 6' 10⅔", and casually went over. Like a magician before his enraptured audience, he kept raising the bar until finishing at 7' 1½", slung his warm-up suit over his shoulder and, whistling, sauntered out of the stadium. Brumel was left flabbergasted, having never even attempted that kind of height during training.

The day of the meet Brumel, like a bride before a wedding, refused to look in Thomas's direction and further shut himself off by reading an adventure novel between attempts. Jumping 6' 6¾", he ran back to his book while fifteen others took their turns going over the bar. Although 6' 9⅛" still presented no problem, by the first attempt at 6' 10¼" his concentration had been so diverted by the novel's plot that he dumped the bar with his chest; on the second, his arms got in the way. In dispelling the tension, he had also managed to undermine his momentum. Realizing the field wasn't meant to be a library, Brumel threw the book aside, circled the jumping sector, knocked off some warm-up jumps, and brazenly looked over at Thomas.

The American was lying on a bench and stretching from time to time as though the battle unfolding around him was of no concern, welcoming his competitors to show what they could do with 7': he had conquered it some thirty-four times. Three Russians accepted the invitation and jumped the height.

Prior to Rome, Thomas had competed only against records. Charles Dumas was already on the decline, and no other strong American jumpers were on the scene. When everyone but the Russians had been eliminated, Thomas realized that this time he faced live opposition: the

Russians were operating as a team. It was a gang-up of three to one.

On the first attempt at 7' $\frac{1}{4}$", the Russians all cleared. Thomas missed but raced back to the approach area. When he found another jumper ahead of him, he asked the officials to allow him his next attempt while he was still hot. They refused. Upset and offended, he stormed out of the jumping area for the opposite corner of the stadium. Watching the whole scene, Brumel realized Thomas wasn't so invincible as he pretended.

Brumel cleared 7' $1\frac{1}{4}$" grazing the bar. He looked up from the landing pit at the quivering crosspiece with a prayer and watched it slowly subside. He lay a few seconds on the shavings, gazing happily into the inky Roman sky.

Thomas jammed into the same height with his whole body and went running from the bar with his head in his hands. He missed the next attempt and was knocked out of the event.

The strong athlete had become a victim of a weak strategy. His first mistake had been his energy-draining show-off training. His second: going overboard in psyching out his opponents by passing up heights and not bothering to limber up between attempts. By the time he finally joined the real struggle, it was too late.

Brumel won the silver medal; Robert Shavlakadze, another Russian, garnered the gold.

Black Thursday, the Americans called it, their odds-on favorite ending up in third place in the greatest upset in Olympic history.

Half a year later at the U.S. Nationals in Madison Square Garden, Thomas and Brumel alone remained in the competition after 7'. Only Thomas and Dumas had jumped the height in American track-and-field history, and the twenty thousand fans whistled a salute to the arrival of a Russian into the club.

In the Soviet Union, people whistle to rag a bad performance. Brumel attributed the crowd's reaction to the cold war and grit his teeth in the resolve to go on with it, regardless. The whistling doubled when he shot over 7' $\frac{1}{2}$". Finally an interpreter translated the American custom, and Brumel flashed his broad, friendly smile.

The Russian's next jump is known today as a straddle-roll classic, an athletic collector's item. He began his run-up relaxed, jogging, and turned on his sprint for the last dozen meters. He looked almost awkward as he ran, his elbows gradually moving forward to balance his torso's backward tilt. At the last moment, his body tightened into a spring and, without losing a fraction of a second in braking, began to kick off. Both arms shot up and his body straightened. His take-off leg, combining a weight lifter's strength and a sprinter's speed, recoiled convulsively. Once in the air, he switched on to automatic flight-control, signaling to every muscle in his body its exact relation to the bar, and passed over. First his curled right leg went over, clearing a fraction of a second faster and preserving the momentum better than the straightened leg of other jumpers. His head went over next, his wide-open mouth dramatically evincing the strain of pushing off.

Next he flung his right arm back like a lever, igniting the second-stage thrust needed to haul the rest of his body over. The moment his left arm had made it, he shifted into stage three by kicking his left leg skyward like a bolt of lightning; this served not only for clearance but also to complete the balancing of his body in flight. The Americans christened the caper the spin-roll, and the Russians rapturously described it as "pouring the body over the bar like a cascade of clear water."

Thomas decided to discard the guise of the carefree superstar and concentrate. He matched Brumel at every height, making everything on the first attempt until 7' 1¾". On the second try, he hesitated in the run-up— meditating, sizing up the bar. Finally he ran. At the last moment, instead of kicking off, he veered unexpectedly. The zigzag was met by unanimous boos, giving Brumel another lesson in the nuances of American behavior.

Athletes are more sensitive to crowd noise in indoor competition than outdoors. Under the added burden of knowing he had four inches on the Russian's 6' ¾" frame, Thomas muffed the jump again. The Garden became a madhouse.

It happened that the meet fell on Thomas's birthday. Brumel, having grown up in a society where "man is a friend, comrade, and brother to his fellow man," resolved to put a stop to the bacchanal: for the first time since they'd begun competing, he walked up to the American and shook his hand. A hush came over the crowd. Brumel wished his rival success for the future and luck on his birthday. The translator plugged into the audience. Stand by stand, the entire Garden took up a resounding chorus of "Happy Birthday."

For the next two years, the Soviet Union and the United States engaged one moment in peaceful démarche and the next in missile crises. Track-and-field diplomacy was the watchword during the thaws.

Brumel and Thomas became friends. In Moscow the American trained with the Russian, visited his home, and barbecued at his dacha. Every Soviet paper used a picture of the two sawing firewood as a symbol of international cooperation.

The son of a mechanic, Brumel had always been told to make something of himself. His parents had pushed him first into art school and, when that failed, had forced him to take up the violin. Though he had never mastered the arts, he idolized artists throughout his teens. As an adult—as a champion—he struck up a friendship with Rostropovich. He met Yevtushenko, Voznesenskii, and Aksënov, through whom he discovered Hemingway, and he hung a portrait in his apartment of Papa wearing a heavy fisherman's knit and a sneer for his effete admirers. Printed in thousands of copies, this picture had become quickly *de rigueur* in the homes of Moscow's intelligentsia. When John Steinbeck came to Moscow, the same fashion-hungry literati stacked their bookshelves with *The Grapes of Wrath* and *Tortilla Flat*, quoting his phrases unctuously in society salons.

Gorky Street was inundated next with the sacred tomes of Faulkner. "One donkey's ass in Faulkner is worth more than all the bridges bombed in Hemingway," quipped a leading critic.

The technocrats of the early sixties were busy reading economists Tereshchenko and Smeliakov on the superiority of American industry. People lined up for blocks for the first American exposition in Sokolniki Park, not only to behold the achievements of capitalism, but with an impudent self-mockery in their eyes, as if to say, "Let's see how America's rubbing our noses in the dirt." These weren't blatant dissidents; like all Russians, they'd never protest anything openly. But they were making a statement just as strong with a perfectly legal visit to an American exhibit.

Workers decorated their walls with the picture of Kennedy that appeared in *Pravda* the day of his funeral. They discovered he was a human being like themselves, with two children and an attractive young wife. After years of Soviet power, Russians had come to expect gray nonpersonalities whose lives lay hidden behind the Kremlin's walls. When they saw that a leader could be young and personable and champion fresh ideas, they hallowed his picture with an honored place on the wall beside their icons.

The romance with America took hold of the masses spontaneously, independent of Khrushchev's politics, though the Premier peppered his speeches with Brumel's name as a password of predétente relations.

By November 1964, after winning meets and breaking world records for three and a half years with the regularity of an assembly line, Brumel felt tired and out of shape. He lost the Soviet championship and was sent to the Tokyo Olympics only out of deference to his prior glories.

In Tokyo the question arose as to how to keep up the façade of the Russian's invincibility and hide what was going on from Thomas until the last minute. This wasn't easy: the athletes had reversed roles since Rome, and the press was now hunting for the Russian. Brumel went to say hello to Thomas at the Olympic stadium and, after signing some autographs, was whisked away in an embassy limousine to Meiji Park to train in an out-of-the-way nook, where, it was thought, not even muggers would bother to intrude.

It was barely an hour before a media landing party came charging out of the bushes, cameras ready. Team director Gavriil Korobkov took down the crossbar and uprights so quickly that not a single reporter discovered Brumel was in bad enough shape two days before the event as to be unable to handle even 6' 7 15/16". Korobkov shut Brumel up in a room with Elmer Martin, his masseur. Instead of kneading the jumper's legs, Martin played chess with him around the clock. Although Brumel was an inveterate player, he had always been an easy mark for Martin. In Tokyo, Martin received a directive to start losing.

Brumel's unexpected run of luck cheered him up. The next morning the Russians ferreted out an abandoned, littered school stadium. Soviet embassy officials stationed themselves as lookouts at the entrance. Brumel jumped 6' 10⅔". Knowing he could usually add another 4 or 5 inches at the real thing, he relaxed in the thought that he was back in shape. But by the time night rolled around he began to tense up again and had trouble falling asleep. Sneaking out of the Olympic Village past the directors and his sleeping roommate, he ducked into the first open bar, downed a full glass of vodka, stole back to his bed, and fell sound asleep.

In the qualifying rounds the next morning, Brumel failed to clear better than 6' 9⅛"—and that only on the third try. "I appealed to God," Brumel recalled. " 'Jesus,' I said, 'why are you doing this to me? I've never done anyone any harm!' " His prayers must have been heard, since somehow he managed the qualifying height. On his way out of the jumping sector he spotted Korobkov, who was aghast, eyes bulging behind his thick glasses at his golden boy. Brumel dashed forward to hide and went crashing headfirst into a low iron gate. "It knocked some sense into me," Brumel said. "Only after hitting it did it occur to me that I had no right to lose to the American."

That evening, after jumping 6' 10¼", Brumel was asked to appear in the officials' quarters: Stig Pettersson, the Swedish jumper, was claiming that Brumel's soles were thicker than regulation. In 1958 another Russian jumper, Yuri Stepanov, had scandalized the sports world after felling the world record while using two-inch soles. The result of extended debates was that his shoes were disallowed, and sole size was limited to half an inch.

Though cracked and patched, Brumel's lucky spikes were perfectly in accordance with the rules. Pettersson had had it in mind to trip up the Russian. Instead, Brumel managed to convert his fury at the accusation into physical power. He cleared 7' 1⅞".

"By the time they set the bar at 7' 2⅝" I was wiped out," Brumel said. "I just knew I couldn't handle the jump. I looked at Thomas and he looked back at me. He seemed up for it, but it was clear that he had had it, too. Right away I knew he couldn't make the height either, that he'd settle for second. He even looked satisfied."

The two sports superpowers silently agreed to put an end to their rivalry, peacefully missed three times each, and embraced. Although physically in worse shape, Brumel won the championship; Thomas got the silver. Their four-year-long competition, which had brought the world bar to 7' 5¾", had come to an end.

Lying with a near-severed foot in Sklifosovskii Hospital, Brumel read the telegram from Boston again and again, unwilling to believe he'd never be able to return to the field and the cheers of the crowd.

Six months and three operations later, in March 1966, Brumel left the hospital with the bone collected and compressed by metal plates and screws supposed to help it knit.

He limped on crutches to a nearby swimming pool. Some of the people standing around lowered him carefully into the water, like a toy into a tub. So as not to be patronized, the next time he used his good leg to push off. A resounding belly flop refractured the bone, and he went for a fourth operation at the world-famous Central Institute of Traumatology and Orthopedics.

Zoia Mironova, an outstanding surgeon, treated the leg with a cast first and later with a steel vice. The leg was propped up and remained suspended, motionless, for weeks. But Mironova assured Brumel it would be worth it: he'd jump again. Reporters heard the prognosis and published the news that Brumel was on the road to recovery. Shrugging, Mironova later admitted to the Sports Committee leaders, "I said it to keep the patient's spirits up. As a physician, I'm not giving any guarantees."

Brumel left the institute with a cane, limping badly, his right leg an inch and a half shorter than his left. He was tired of doctors, and they were as tired of him. His wife, Valentina, who had come almost grudgingly to the stadium, even when she knew he was going to try to break a record, asked for a separation: "You've slept with half the Sports Institute and every one of your nurses, and the whole miserable thing began after that damned rendezvous with Tamara." A divorce seemed inevitable. Valentina got the apartment, furnished in elegant Petersburg antiques. Brumel loaded his favorite Fabergé samovar into the Mercedes and moved into a rented room.

Coach Diachkov, who had shared Brumel's greatest triumphs, was busy with a crop of healthy young jumpers and had no time to see him. Friends drifted away and newspapers lost interest in the man to whom they'd once devoted miles of copy. The few people that stuck with him felt sorry for him personally but considered him washed up as an athlete.

By 1968, Brumel's leg had not only not knitted but began to develop osteomyelitis. Valerii took his pills with vodka. "I just couldn't imagine what I'd do without sports. I went around with the vision of an abyss before me. Sometimes I felt like flinging myself out of a window head-first and ending it all." The idea of suicide became more persistent when Brumel heard that a Japanese marathoner he'd met at Tokyo had committed harakiri after breaking his leg and becoming convinced he'd never run again.

When someone phoned anonymously and referred the jumper to a surgeon in the backwater burg of Kurgan who could heal any break and perform assorted other miracles, Brumel was skeptical. Still, he called the doctor, one Ilizarov, who seemed amazed the athlete hadn't come to him sooner. Two hours later, Brumel was winging his way to Siberia.

Gavriil Ilizarov, a man with a large face and the bushy mustache of a Red Cavalry officer, claimed he had gone into medicine to eliminate deformity. His first step was to reject the time-honored practice of using a cast for fractures.

According to Ilizarov, the slightest jarring shifts the two pieces of a broken bone inside a cast and prevents the bone from knitting. Instead of a cast, he designed a simple apparatus consisting of two to four rings sporting spokes to be driven through the soft tissues of the bone. The rings are joined together by threaded rods that can be moved together or apart as desired. The process of fixing the bone consists of tightening the spokes and rods, thereby compressing the two halves of the bone.

In addition, Ilizarov's apparatus disproved the notion that adult human bone can no longer grow—at least not sufficiently to achieve the necessary results. By leaving, say, a one-inch gap between the two halves of a broken bone and then, as the growing tissue fills this space, regulating the gap with the screws, he found he could add literally inches. The following examples of Ilizarov's work are *not* science fiction:

• He operated on a man who'd been born with one leg shorter than the other and then used the apparatus to add nearly 10 inches.

• In a man with a congenitally dislocated hip, the femur stuck nearly 5 inches out of its socket. The man stood doubled over, unable to sit, his sciatic nerve pinched. His face was a mask of suffering. Ilizarov closed the dislocation and aligned the femur, turning a 5'5" freak into a handsome, well-built 5' 10".

• Ilizarov's apparatus straightened badly bowed legs, cured chronic contracture, and . . . salvaged a marriage: the bride, a head taller than the groom and a bit mindless, had herself shortened 4 inches for the sake of her spouse.

• In the middle of 1969 Dmitri Shostakovich began feeling a numbing of the extremities. The most outstanding physicians in Moscow believed the condition to be neurological and progressive, and gave him no more than a year. His fourteenth symphony became a meditation on death. Minister of Culture Ekaterina Furtseva, who had learned of Ilizarov through Rostropovich, had the miracle worker flown in to examine the composer. The doctor offered another diagnosis and performed an operation in Kurgan, where he used his apparatus to provide transverse tension on the vertebrae. Shostakovich lived another six years and died of a heart attack in 1975.

(Ilizarov spent eighteen years fighting for recognition of his methods by the Soviet medical establishment, which had branded him a charlatan. The Brumel case at last brought him publicity; recently a clinic was built in Kurgan where Ilizarov and dozens of his students are now busy with more than a hundred variants of the original apparatus in ever more fantastic cases.)

Brumel's operation consisted of cutting the broken bone across the old fracture and under the knee (where, Ilizarov was convinced, there is a special regenerative zone).

Ideally, a leg in a cast shouldn't be moved for three or four months. In three or four months the prostrate patient develops bedsores and a bad mood and still occasionally upsets the leg. With Ilizarov's method, the patient begins walking on crutches the day after the operation, slowly increasing the load on the bone and facilitating its growth.

Within two weeks Brumel had given up his crutches and begun perambulating the corridors with a cane. Ilizarov assured him that the leg would never break again in the same place.

Four months later, free of the cane, Brumel stepped off a plane in Moscow and planted two legs of equal length squarely on the ground. Behind him lay seven major operations, twenty-five lesser ones, and 1,468 days of wandering from hospital to hospital.

At an empty gym again for the first time since the accident, Brumel's atrophied muscles failed to negotiate a mere 4' 11", a height he had jumped as a thirteen-year-old. Ashamed to be seen among athletes, he spent the next months running up and down the staircases of his twelve-story building—not especially noteworthy to the neighbors, who often did the same whenever the elevator broke down.

Finally he returned to the gym, but he'd either brush the bar with his hand or pull Thomas-like zigzags, psychologically unready to signal sufficient lift. He left the gym feeling he could never jump again, after all—that he'd been better off in the hospital, where at least he had consoled himself with illusions.

At home again, he placed a record distractedly on his Philips stereo. An old Sinatra tune bathed him in nostalgia. Never bothering much with the lyrics, for the first time he tried to make out the words. They spoke of the dark of a storm, the wind and the rain. And they spoke of walking through it with one's head held high.

He listened to the song again and again. Suddenly he leaped across the room like a dancer, grabbed the record from the turntable, and raced to the car. In the gym half an hour later, Sinatra-inspired, he hit 5′ 10⅞″.

Once again Brumel became busy with calculations and diagrams, debates with his new trainer, Yuri Chistiakov, and detailed plans for getting into shape for the European championships.

On March 13, 1969, he invited a dozen of his closest friends to an exhibition at the Young Pioneer Stadium. More than three hundred showed up. He reached 6′ 7½″, but it savored of a satisfaction greater than that of a new world record. He took off his spikes—the old lucky shoes, holes and all—and kissed them.

Brumel took third place at the Moscow championships in May with 6′ 9½″ and contentedly looked over the table he'd drawn up:

	1963	*1969*
Age	21	27
Pulse	82	80
Pressure	120/80	120/80
Arm strength	78 kg	90 kg
Squat with snatch	175 kg	165 kg
100-meter dash	10.5 sec	11.1 sec
Jerk	100 kg	100 kg
Pole vault	13′ 9¼″	13′ 1¾″
Long jump	25′ 1¼″	24′ 4¼″
High jump	7′ 5¾″	6′ 9½″

Asked about Brumel's prospects, a Sports Committee official commented, "None. He'll never do 7′ 5¾″ again, and I doubt he'll hit even 7′. Maybe 6′ 10⅝″. But no one cares about that these days—neither us nor him."

Who is Brumel, really? A man with an ape's instincts who can't live without jumping? A stubborn fool who's happy only when defying fate or meeting a challenge? An ambitious upstart who breathes in glory like oxygen? All of these, perhaps. The least that can be said is that his life has added a human touch to the tough world of sports. And not only to sports.

Throughout the sixties, Brumel would return to Voroshilovgrad to appear before the workers. He'd speak to overflowing auditoriums in poetic phrases of the grandeur of Communism and the motherland, which had given him the strength and inspiration to compete in stadiums all over the world and made him proud now to recount his victories before the people. In truth, Brumel was coming to buy $6,000 cars from the provincial party committee's warehouse for $18,000 resales to Georgian tycoons. (Valerii enjoyed the good life as much as the next man, and he was just as willing to use a political front to maintain it.)

In 1968 the International Olympic Committee invited Brumel as an honorary guest to the Mexico City Olympics. He accepted, carrying an elegant cane with silver inlay.

No longer competing and no longer invited on speaking tours, Valerii was badly in need of money. But more than money, he missed the risk, the breathtaking adventure, of competition. He replaced track-and-field events with smuggling, stashing a rumored $5,000 into the bottom of the hollow cane and screwing the simple metal cap back on. He was caught by customs in front of hundreds of passengers at Sheremetevo airport.

Possession of dollars in the USSR is punishable by eight years, but so overwhelming were his services considered that the Kremlin swiftly gave the word not only to let him go but also, in order to kill any gossip, to have him publish a by-lined article in *Pravda* on the Soviet team's chances in Mexico City.

In 1974 Brumel wrote a novel about scientists, and he has since gotten a doctorate in sports psychology. Today, at thirty-five, Valerii Brumel has not yet lost his *joie de vivre*, his sense of life as a boundlessly fascinating experiment.

THREE

Daredevil Gymnastics

July 22, 1976: the Olympic women's all-around gymnastics competition was under way at the Montreal Forum.

Proud little Olga Korbut, red-pigtailed and ideally proportioned, was last to approach the uneven parallels. She paused, drew herself up coquettishly to her full height of five feet, surveyed the audience, gaily waved her hand to someone, and mischievously winked.

But Olga didn't look well. She seemed pale, her eyes sunken and her cheekbones too prominent. There had been two restless nights. Sedatives, even had they been allowed, would have offered too little too late: by the opening of the Olympics she was on the verge of breakdown.

From the age of eleven, Olga Korbut had worked toward victory, rushing through endless Soviet and European championships, World Cups and international meets, Spartacus Games and pre-Olympic trials, each time stretching herself to the limit, hurling her body from apparatus to apparatus, exploding with pyrotechnical stunts. Between meets she had disposed decisively of anyone in her way.

Now, midway through the events at Montreal, Olga found herself at odds with her coach, Renald Knysh, senior coach Larisa Latynina, and perhaps the whole of the Soviet Union. Her own teammates had branded her a know-it-all and a petty tyrant—shamelessly bourgeois.

This was not the first time Olga had gotten herself into trouble: three years earlier she had unexpectedly refused to go on an exhibition tour to the United States.

The typical U.S. tour is made up of one day apiece in ten to twelve cities: ten to twelve sold-out performances of a set of four of the riskiest routines in gymnastics. A day in a gymnast's life on the road consists of airport, performance, lunch, bus, performance, airport; how many times could she demonstrate a faultless backwards somersault on the beam or a daring full-twisting Tsukahara on the horse, knowing that the hundreds of thousands in profits would be split entirely between the Soviet government and the American promoter? The performers never saw a cent.

"I want to buy presents for my sisters, cousins, nieces, uncles, parents," Olga declared.

The declaration sent shock waves through the Moscow sports establishment: members of the Soviet national teams are assumed to regard a trip abroad itself as an otherwise unavailable privilege, the bonus that supplements their monthly stipend ($400 to $550 in gymnastics and weight lifting; $300 in volleyball). Officially, an athlete's service is identical with that of any other toiler of socialism. An increased stipend is out of the question.

Olga had simply recognized gymnastics exhibitions for

what they are—a commercial show—and dared to follow the example of her Western counterparts.

She was warned that she faced not only expulsion from the National Team but outright retirement from gymnastics. "See if I care," she taunted, knowing full well that the team contract with the American promoter was binding only if she was on the tour.

Following a series of trans-Atlantic negotiations, Olga was informed that she could visit the department store of her choice and take home all the gifts she could carry. (Considering her size, neither the Soviet government nor the American promoter was likely to go bankrupt.)

On another occasion, her face a mixture of pain and petulance, Olga had complained of a sprained shoulder and asked to cancel her tour. The shoulder was palpated and X-rayed; half a dozen doctors found nothing. "Well," she said with a shrug, "I'll go . . . if my coach goes too."

Shuffling trips abroad like notebooks in her schoolbag, manipulating the National Team's training schedule to suit herself, venturing to quit the platform in the middle of an international meet between the USSR, Finland, and Hungary, Olga was unsettling Soviet philosophy with an alien concept: personality. It wasn't long before the mere mention of her name made athletic directors recoil.

"It's hard to fight Olga," said one Soviet official in the stands of the Montreal Forum. "The President of the United States himself receives her."

"The West will support Olga. The audience is going to be with her," said another.

The women's all-around competition is a two-hour contest in which the participants battle the beam, the bars,

the vaulting horse, and the floor exercise; the highest total
score determines the queen of gymnastics. In Munich the
crown had been captured by Liudmila Turishcheva. Now,
in Montreal, Turishcheva's face, still a stranger to cos-
metics at twenty-four, looked the color of alabaster, like
that of one of Tolstoi's noblewomen—in leotards, instead
of crinoline. Only after her warm-up on the horse, as she
returned to her place frowning, clenching her teeth,
tightening her lips, did a hint of color appear on her
cheeks.

When the Soviets arrived in Montreal Liudmila had
been the happiest woman on the team. At a general gather-
ing of the Soviet delegation she had made the following
speech: "Hockey player Boris Mikhailov has handed me a
hockey stick autographed by the winners of the Innsbruck
Olympics. I think of it as a relay baton; I swear, on behalf
of our entire team, to give my all to win."

A member of the Central Committee of the Young Communist League (Komsomol), the top of the Soviet youth
hierarchy, Liudmila valued her gymnastic achievements
not so much for her own sake as for "cementing Communism." She measured happiness by the pleasure she
brought to others, whether her schoolmates or all 270
million of her countrymen. No other athlete so completely
enjoyed the confidence of the Training Council (the gov-
erning body of Soviet gymnastics).

Then, two days before the Games began, the Training
Council met to designate a team captain. After weighing
the pros and cons till 3 A.M., the officials and coaches opted
to sacrifice the undefeated, dependable Turishcheva and
install Korbut instead. It was clear that it had not been
the two gymnasts' competitive merits but Olga's worldwide
celebrity that had prompted the strategy.

Liudmila was stunned. Just when she had been feeling readier than ever for the fight the Council had abandoned her, with Senior Coach Latynina admonishing her to forget what happened for the sake of the team.

Such a blow might have been easier to absorb during her debut at the world championship in Ljubljana seven years before, when Liudmila was used to open the competition. It's taken for granted that the first competitor is given the lowest scores, regardless of the quality of her performance: the history of women's gymnastics shows that such "icebreakers" have typically been sacrificed for the interests of the team. Liudmila was the exception: in 1969, pegged as the inexperienced underdog, she not only broke the ice but melted the hearts of the judges as well, who acknowledged her all-around champion of the world.

Since Ljubljana, Liudmila had been assigned last place on the team, as its captain—the positional arithmetic revealing an understanding between judges and trainers that a team's last performer is its signature. Judges tend automatically to give her the highest scores and accept her as the favorite in future all-around competitions.

After the vote in Montreal Liudmila discovered the pain of betrayal. Her strong arms were tense; her fists, clenched. For a moment they fell to her sides, suddenly soft and rounded. Then again the muscles stiffened, as though ready to slug their way to the title.

Forty-one-year-old Larisa Latynina, the blond, gray-eyed senior coach of the National Team, turned back to look at her girls along the edges of the Forum. Not one had been her own pupil. Possessor of a still-unsurpassed nineteen Olympic and world championship gold medals, she now found herself with a gaggle of unruly wards boasting trainers of their own—all men—and making it clear they did nothing more than tolerate her presence.

Mme. Berthe Villanche, the French strongwoman in charge of the Women's Technical Committee of the International Gymnastics Federation, had outlawed all men— including judges, in effect—from anywhere in or near the performance area. Relegated to the training halls alone, the men went on teaching the girls their "unfeminine" gimmickry unimpeded. Paradoxically, Latynina's visible activity had thereby been reduced to virtual housekeeping, carrying stools submissively to and from the platform.

Powerless though she may have been during the contest, Latynina had been influential in the selection of the team: she had demanded inclusion of girls who had come in below third in the pre-Olympic trials and rejected others more worthy. At the Training Council conference she was informed that she had brought the wrong team to Montreal.

The tone of the conference was set by the head of the Soviet Sports Committee's gymnastics division, Yuri Titov, a broad-shouldered, clean-cut man with a fistful of Olympic medals of his own. (Titov had just been elected president of the International Gymnastics Federation, defeating perennial president Arthur Gander of Switzerland by a narrow 26–25 margin.) The argument was raised that Latynina had left behind Shaposhnikova and Davydova, both more competent and no less confident than the amazing Rumanian Comaneci. Latynina's chief sin, it was explained, was in stubbornly refusing to forsake her "classical" gymnastics tradition for the "athletic" school, which offered dazzling point-producing maneuvers.

From 1954 to 1966 Latynina had herself been unequaled

as a competitor in world gymnastics, winning with programs that excelled in grace and lyricism. Each of her movements showed the elegance and refinement she had always admired in the Bolshoi Ballet. She was the quintessential classicist.

Then, at the Tokyo Olympics, Latynina was outmatched by the unknown Vera Caslavska of Czechoslovakia. For six months the upset was attributed to chance—until fifteen-year-old Larisa Petrik became all-around champion of the Soviet Union.

Judges and officials everywhere began speaking of the new "athletic" style, which consisted of extremely complex, rapid-fire routines. International gymnastics symposium-goers talked of the Burda Twirl (after the Russian Liuba Burda, who executed a 720-degree turn on the uneven parallels), the Yamashita (after Haruhiro Yamashita's handspring-push-off and post-flight pike-and-extend from the horse), Korbut's Element (a backwards aerial on the beam), the Tsukahara (after the Japanese Mitsuko Tsukahara, who performed a vaulting somersault with a 180-degree twist), and Ultra-C (unusually complex combinations).

If she accepted this daredevil virtuosity intellectually, Latynina remained fondest of a style formed of cameos and études. And in the midst of the stampede to athleticism she had had the nerve to write that "teaching complicated maneuvers is easier than developing a motif. . . . The former is the beginning of the end of femininity, without which I can't conceive of women's gymnastics."

She went on to complain that "nowadays the stunt is no longer bound up with the composition as a whole. It's the thing that attracts attention: 'How did she manage it? Why didn't she fall?' Should such somersaults then be abandoned? No, but the tricks must be transformed into components of the exercise."

At the Training Council conference Latynina's notions were denounced and her attempts to integrate the two styles declared ineffective.

The day of the all-around competition, Nadia Comaneci found herself in Turishcheva's group. Occasionally she'd glance at her formidable rival, but mostly, with her slender, shapely legs and dainty, pointed shoulders, she hopped around like a sparrow. Yet a woman's grace emerged the moment she broke into a warm-up run. Her profile—brow, nose, lips, chin—seemed as if sketched in one swift flourish by an artist who had discarded the softness of childhood and focused only on the stark determination of the athlete.

Nadia has been described as fearless. If that is so, it may be only because she has never had to clash with fear. From the age of six her supple, responsive body has grown accustomed to rotating, twisting, executing prodigious feats—feats no gymnast of eighteen or nineteen would dare, much less be able, to perform.

The weight of a child is evenly distributed, with a superior strength-to-weight ratio. As a teenage girl matures, her weight moves down to her hips. With each year the young star, though on the strictest of diets, finds herself a little bit larger, a little bit heavier; the process of growing up is relentless. At each jump her muscles, ligaments, and tendons are subjected to considerably greater loads—and therefore to injury. Even a minor muscle tear or sprained joint forces the gymnast to be more cautious, thriftier with herself.

Nadia doesn't know the meaning of a calculated risk.

She was simply born to be a gymnast. She burst into the world of athletic competition, as Mozart did in music, to occupy the place reserved for genius.

The Soviet populace is exhorted to begin gymnastics from birth. Mothers are taught to give bending and stretching exercises to their month-old infants. Every morning at six-thirty, Moscow radio and television begin their broadcasting day exclaiming, "Good morning, comrades! We shall now begin our gymnastics class . . ."

According to official statistics, nine million workers lock their lathes, shut down their conveyors, and drop their welding torches every day at eleven to enjoy ten minutes of squats and leg raises so that they can go back to work refreshed and double their output. In theory, gymnastics accompanies every Soviet citizen through life; just before a Russian takes his last breath, one would expect him to jump up, do an exercise, and settle back quietly to die.

Moscow boasts the greatest number of children involved in gymnastics. Tens of thousands of six- and seven-year-olds master the exercises. At eight they enter public school, where they develop their talents under the supervision of a phys. ed. instructor. Later the most talented are enrolled in state-subsidized sports associations with intensive training programs, such as the Central Army Club, which has eighteen gyms and whose coaches all hold diplomas from the Moscow Central Institute of Sports and Physical Culture and know the latest tricks of the trade. Many have doctorates in their field.

Yet in the last ten years Moscow coaches, as well as those of Leningrad and Kiev (the other citadels of mass gymnastics), have failed to produce a single outstanding gymnast. All great Soviet gymnasts traditionally have hailed from smaller provincial towns where gymnastics is the least popular of sports and the gyms are littered with crumbling plaster and old apparatus. It was Grodno, for example, located on the Western frontier of the USSR, and Groznyi, lost in the mountains of the northern Caucasus, that produced Olga Korbut and Liudmila Turishcheva, respectively.

After the close of every Olympic Games, grand symposiums are held for days at a time in Moscow at which coaches from all over the country are told "What Is to Be Done"—a question that has confronted Russians since well before the Bolshevik Revolution. In 1968 the slogan was "Every sports school must cultivate its own Liuba Burda." In 1972 this was formulated more harshly: "A gymnastics coach can justify his salary only by producing his own Olga Korbut." No doubt the participants in the 1976 symposium were harangued to search for a Nadia Comaneci.

That the USSR has 150,000 talented teenagers engaged exclusively in gymnastics does not guarantee gold medals. The eight million athletes involved in Russian winter sports are double the entire population of Norway, a country that earned more gold medals than did the USSR at Grenoble in 1968 and took first place in team competitions. Numbers do not breed excellence. What it takes is a unique individual with an instinctive feeling for sports, one whose ideas about gymnastics are at once so new and so mad that he is able to detonate veritable human fireworks.

In Grodno, such an individual proved to be Renald Knysh, a self-taught inventor with a flair for welding wings to man. In Groznyi, it was Vladislav "Iron Jaw"

Rastorotskii, an amateur psychologist with a curiosity about creating a machine out of a twelve-year-old girl.

It was 4:30 P.M. when Korbut approached the bars. She looked at the apparatus as if to charm it into submission. Taking hold of the lower bar, she began. The essence of the event lies in motion: the gymnast is allowed to hold no more than three positions—and then only in order to concentrate briefly before a difficult element.

In recent years the athleticists have encouraged a squall of uninterrupted Ultra-C elements, making performances impressive but slick. What Olga did flashed by in a shower of red, the rebellious color of her leotard. To the sound of thousands of clicking cameras she soared between the bars, barely grazing them with her hands. She stood momentarily on the upper bar, and in an instant she seemed to plummet hopelessly; she swirled in a sharp arc, only to clutch the upper bar again and position herself magically parallel to the floor and perpendicular to the apparatus.

A victorious 9.90 flashed across the scoreboard. Her bold new handstand and staggering display had surpassed even her show in Munich four years before.

Olga sat on the floor swinging her leg loosely from side to side. She looked at the rapturously applauding audience, examining them like a general inspecting his ranks before the next attack.

Olga had recently acquired a more sophisticated approach to gymnastics: "Medals and titles don't do anything for me anymore. The audience's love is what I'm fighting for. When I'm loosening up before going out onto the platform, I'm already aware of how the crowd feels toward me. If I establish contact I'm guaranteed success. But if the faces in the stands are stern, even if they're only indifferent, my spirit plunges. I just love it when the fans go wild with applause. Sometimes I want their palms to crack from clapping."

If Olga had failed to blister their hands, she surely had captured their hearts. Still, she looked tense. Wearing a warm-up suit, she strode along the narrow passageway in front of the other girls, did a few somersaults, and stopped at the water cooler. She took off her pants and jacket and, moistening her fingers, washed the chalk off her leotard, legs, neck, and hands. She fluffed her bangs and, like Cinderella, turned from a grim servant of the apparatus into a naughty but winsome little girl. Her fatigue had melted away.

Moving forward again, occasionally by somersault, she found a boxlike object behind the bench. She laid her jacket on it and sat facing the audience, an actress keeping photographers busy as well as an athlete needing distraction from her tension.

The all-around Olympic championship was her big chance to vanquish Turishcheva. Olga had always been charged up for spectacular shows in one or two gymnastic events but vulnerable in lengthier competitions, and she yearned to prove herself in the longer haul. Though fired with the flames of ambition, she had been beaten by Liudmila at every all-around in their eight years of rivalry.

Pugnacious as a teenager and jealous as a woman, Olga would try to curb her emotions and then vent them at Liudmila—a small measure of revenge for her constant frustration.

"Of course," sniped Olga in an interview with *Komsomolskaia Pravda*, "it's easy to wag your arms and legs a bit more accurately. But then you can't break away. You get the dumb medal and you don't let anyone down. We've got a gymnast or two who are still like that."

At the 1973 USSR championship Olga refused to shake Liudmila's hand on the winner's platform.

Before the exhibition tour to the United States in 1974, she complained that the two of them were incompatible and asked that they be separated. Liudmila was sent on tour to Australia.

In response to a Soviet TV interviewer's question about which of her rivals would take the all-around championship, she swiped—knowing full well that Liudmila was current champion—"Somebody good at complicated routines. The Rumanian girl, Nadia Comaneci."

Until Montreal, Olga and Nadia had never met in competition. In part, this had been a tactical move on the part of the Training Council, which felt that a pre-Olympic loss to Nadia might upset Olga at the Games.

As a rival, Nadia didn't scare Olga in the least. The Rumanian was just an object of curiosity—as such, psychologically ideal for a sports contest. Liudmila, on the other hand, was more than concrete—a wall against which Olga's attacks bounced off like tennis balls. Olga found nothing more infuriating.

Olga looked at the entrance to the locker room. Knysh, the man she needed, wasn't there. Before departing for Montreal, the gymnast and her trainer had gotten into a fight. In a fit of anger Olga had blurted, "You're making a bundle off of me!" Knysh had stayed behind in Grodno.

An Honored Coach of the USSR and director of a gymnastics school, Renald Knysh receives a monthly salary of

$300 (the average is $180). In addition, he receives numerous allowances from the town fathers of Grodno, a city rescued from provincial obscurity by its gymnastic achievements. As the coach who forged in Olga a two-time champion of the Soviet Union and three-time winner of the Olympic gold medal in individual and team competition, Knysh was also entitled to official awards from the Soviet government ranging from $500 to $1500.

Was Olga right to accuse him as she had? Is it wrong for a person to make money coaching? To a Westerner the question makes no sense. To Russians, on the other hand, "profiteering" is the line that separates the good guys (those who work mainly for the sake of higher values and very little to fill their own coffers) from the bad guys (who find a fast buck in everything).

Olga is herself an advanced entrepreneur; what she said to Knysh was only spit out in anger. She knew better than anyone else that her coach never took a cent for himself but invested everything he had in the construction of a gym. The town fathers, though claiming support for the famous trainer, considered his project—the first in the world for teaching grandiose acrobatics (for Knysh, gymnastics meant acrobatics on apparatus)—the fancy of eccentric genius. They declined to donate a kopeck toward its construction.

The thirty-seven-year-old Knysh, 6'2" with kind eyes and closely cropped black hair, organized his students into a construction brigade. They found a bombed-out bread factory and worked around the clock to clear away the debris. Since trucks were unavailable, Knysh carted over the beams, planks, and bricks in his Zhiguli compact.

Walls up and award funds nearly depleted, Knysh suddenly discovered that roofing materials were unavailable for love or money. The project was dropped, the uprights left thrusting forlornly into the sky. Knysh turned to other matters.

The ideal distance between the uneven parallels differs for every gymnast and, at one time, every girl in training had to struggle with a crank to regulate it. Knysh devised an ingenious system for adjusting the bars: the gymnast looks at a scale, finds her division, and turns a lever to it; the bars are adjusted automatically.

After he found himself too busy spotting his pupils to do anything else, like little more than an insurance agent, Knysh had the floor carpeted with thick felt mats. His gymnasts were guaranteed soft landings.

Like his other projects, working with Olga was Knysh's way of beating back the bleak environment. He developed new stunts. The backwards somersault on the balance beam was not only complicated and risky; it was unheard of. But Knysh had found exactly what he wanted: a girl who considered his stunts the adventure of a lifetime. Together they stunned the sports world.

To keep stunning the sports world, however, was another matter. Knysh engineered a double somersault with pirouettes for the floor exercise which broke every existing canon.

Gymnastics training was once not unlike the training of animals. The coach would suggest a combination of movements and the gymnast would try again and again to execute it. At each attempt the brain sends signals to the muscles as though impelling them to remember the maneuvers. Multiple repetition gives rise to a dynamic reflex, so that the gymnast can perform the entire set of motions automatically.

Knysh believed that progress in gymnastics would be

possible only if, instead of working on a fixed pattern, the athlete created hundreds of variants by tacking on conscious aerial maneuvers. Accordingly, the coach predetermined the specific points in space at which the gymnast would switch on conscious control and orient herself for the rotations to follow. Olga was eager to give it a try.

After a thousand failed attempts she complained to her trainer that his idea had been pure fantasy. Besides, she said, it was *her* body, and she knew best how to use it. Without arguing, Knysh watched as Olga dashed out of the hall, slamming the door behind her. Camped outside were a couple of newspapermen, a BBC television crew, a bunch of autograph hounds, and a contingent of representatives from the local chemical factory who wanted her to share the glory of her Olympic victories with the working classes. The relationship worsened.

Finally Olga stopped training altogether. She would change dresses every two hours, pose, lunch, party, talk of faraway places, expatiate upon the directions in which the world of gymnastics was supposed to be heading. Slowly she forgot how a balance beam and parallel bars even looked.

At a Kremlin reception to award her the Order of the Badge of Honor, reporters asked Knysh whether he was happy with Olga's success.

"No. She didn't do half of what we were working on."

"And the half I *did* do was no thanks to you!" Olga snapped back.

The relationship had hit rock bottom. Yet suddenly conciliatory messages to Knysh began appearing in the press. "A lot of people think our experiments are incompatible with gymnastics," Olga would tell reporters, though still out of training and lounging in a Moscow hotel or an Aeroflot jet. "Others forbid risky routines. Some write theses on the subject. But we just go on training. And we always prove the skeptics wrong."

At last the runaway reappeared in Grodno. She walked quietly into the gym, eyes lowered, avoiding her trainer. Without a word she mounted the bars. Balancing on her stomach, she arched her back and drew her legs slowly up and around until they hung over her slender shoulders and framed her face—the most difficult of all poses in gymnastics. Her features were contorted with pain.

Before the Montreal Olympics Knysh began keeping a close eye on Olga's weight, refusing to allow the addition of even an ounce to her 93 pounds. At one point, in the resort city of Sochi, the women's gymnastics team was eating in a fancy restaurant where some tables had been set with juicy red steaks cooked for a team of soccer players. Sick of her yogurt diet, Olga quickly cased the room, grabbed a steak, and wolfed it down. Then she rushed into the bathroom and, businesslike, inserted two fingers into her throat, throwing up the whole block of meat into the sink. She then reentered the dining room, an obedient child under the fatherly eye of her coach.

At the Forum, when the group that included Turish-cheva and Comaneci approached the uneven bars, a man in a dark blue training suit stood in the corner just behind the barrier. With a flattened nose and broad shoulders, his entire person radiated decisiveness. Vladislav "Iron Jaw" Rastorotskii was the fifty-one-year-old coach of Liudmila Turishcheva.

Rastorotskii had worked as a stoker on a locomotive in

his youth, and he knew one principle well: for a locomotive to move, the furnace must continuously be fed with coal. When he became a trainer, he adapted furnace mechanics to gymnastics. He trained Liudmila to think of her blisters as gems and of 5 A.M. warm-ups as the cornerstone of life. He taught her to mark the passage of time by the number of gym shoes worn out and leotards torn through.

Every boy in Groznyi took pleasure in Liudmila's good looks, but only from a distance: "Iron Jaw" had threatened to castrate anyone who touched her. To facilitate the execution of his threat, he installed her in an apartment next to his own.

Rastorotskii had told his wife he wanted no children, since children might distract him. People who know the man describe him as a once kind, cheerful, and sociable fellow who has been strangely transformed during the last ten years under the stress of coaching. It might as easily be said, on the other hand, that he found his real identity only after meeting Liudmila.

"Talent in gymnastics is for the birds. Self-discipline is everything," he declared. And he proved it: Liudmila has learned the most difficult moves in gymnastics, and learned them without mistakes. She was never a pioneer, but always a perfectionist. In sports this is often rewarded with the title of champion.

As a child, Liudmila had been spotted by Iron Jaw for her unsmiling face and broad forehead. In Montreal, at twenty-four, her face was severe and sublimely aloof, with the expressionlessness of a machine. But her body, with its long legs, supple waist, and shapely breasts, belied the image of cold asceticism.

If Liudmila had forced herself to put aside her hurt at

being displaced as team captain, she was powerless to change the age of her body. When she performed, the bars creaked plaintively or scraped sharply, as if begging to be treated a little easier. But Liudmila could no longer answer its warning signals. Her exercise was complicated and accurate, but it lacked the flavor of flight.

Descending from the platform, Liudmila glanced toward the side of the arena. A fight was going on. A policeman was insisting that Rastorotskii, who had managed to slip across the barrier, leave the area. Iron Jaw pointed to his trainer's suit, lettered CCCP. The policeman seemed unimpressed. Rastorotskii started to lie down on the floor in defiant protest. The policeman summoned a colleague.

Rastorotskii tried to explain: Liudmila's muscles awaited his words, or at least his signs, to function properly. It was how she had been trained for years. Rastorotskii's plea failed to convince the imperturbable cops. Slowly and steadily they escorted him to the exit.

Liudmila smiled, a mixture of sadness and sympathy. She peered at Nadia, who was deftly wiping the upper bars and raising small clouds of chalk dust. Then she removed her barrette. The hair cascaded around her neck in a thick, chestnut-colored fan. Like a girl preparing for a date, she stuck the barrette in her mouth and began combing her hair.

Before another hour had passed, Liudmila had lost the beam to Nadia Comaneci and the floor exercise to Nelli Kim. Later, at a press conference, she said, sniffling, "My sports days are over." The Rastorotskii theory made no allowances for emotional display. But the tears that ran down Liudmila's face in the arena and were wiped away in the corridors of the Forum burst forth anew in her room at the Olympic Village. The automaton, the product of years of brutal crafting, had finally cracked.

Nadia Comaneci puffed on her hands as if to cool them, grabbed the bars, and flowed into them like a moving part of the apparatus. The sulky sparrow was once again metamorphosed into a firebird that could flutter like a butterfly, jump like a squirrel, and swoop like an eagle. She received a perfect 10. The papers described the moment as the fatal blow delivered to the defending champion, Olga, in a four-round bout. The TV cameras followed Olga intimately, as though a glimpse back at Nadia meant a smashing right in retaliation.

In the corridor, a reporter accosted one of the judges.

"How would you describe Comaneci as a human being?" he asked.

"Oh! She's charming," answered the judge with a smile. Nadia's dolls and hobbies were discussed, along with her diet, her spats with her younger brother, and her crush on Alain Delon—and not a thing came across of what she was really like.

The crowds at the Forum were delighted to have witnessed the birth of a new star. Still, enchanted as they may have been with Nadia's technique, their hearts remained Olga's. They needed visual drama to know the human being.

Olga's efforts to subdue the balance beam seemed to result alternately in gold medals and brain concussions.

The event requires that the gymnast demonstrate a torrent of turns, jumps, and running steps on a 16′-by-4″ piece of wood, making sure to use its entire length and distributing difficult elements logically throughout the routine. The performance must offer rhythm and variety, like a small musical piece in which pianissimo, staccato, and crescendo end in a final beat of a kettledrum. For all a gymnast's Ultra-C exercises, the slightest hesitation before any one of them lowers the score.

Olga prepared a routine whose key measures were calculated to make the public gasp, "She's falling!" Indeed, at home her exercises often did end in a fall. Either one leg would miss the beam after a backwards somersault, or her whole body would begin to totter, no longer concerned with rhythm but simply with staying on.

In September 1975, participating in the USSR championships, Olga suffered her third concussion after a fall from the beam. Bloodied and unconscious, she was rushed to the hospital. After coming to, the first thing she wanted to know was how many bloodstains there were on her leotard, as if to make sure she could continue the exercise. When she was released from the hospital thirty-five days later, she announced to reporters, "That's it. I'm leaving sports for good!" Yet after two weeks without training, she surprised the crowds by not only appearing in London for the World Cup but winning the silver medal in the all-around. Asked why she had come to London without having fully recuperated, she replied, "They made me." The "they" she referred to were the aging villains with bulging bellies and bald heads that run the Sports Committee of the USSR on the fifth floor of No. 4 Skatertnaia Street in Moscow.

Are "they" really exploiters who force young talents to compete overseas? Soviet sports executives don't have to push athletes into the international arena. Olga, for example, was considered an annoyance anyway. Refusal on her part would have meant that she'd be officially forgotten, in accordance with the socialist principle that no one is indispensable. But that's inducement enough. Under no circumstances would the Soviet star have wished to return to the status of simple Soviet comrade. To one who has basked in fame, a future as a schoolteacher looks less than unalluring.

Olga sent feelers out indicating an interest in a spot with the school of the Moscow Art Theater. Her hints went unanswered: the Moscow theatrical establishment has an understandable suspicion of eccentric young celebrities. But even had Olga made it to the stage, would she have been satisfied? Jaunts abroad are not readily granted to actors. Instead of her two-bedroom showcase apartment in Grodno, all she could count on in Moscow would have been an overcrowded dorm room; she'd have had no place to hang her fox fur coat from New York and not a free corner for her Grundig stereo from Munich—not to mention that her Arpège perfume from Paris would no doubt have been borrowed by her roommates. A beginning actor's inflexible $100 monthly salary is all that would have awaited her, plus potato and meat lines after rehearsal. If she managed the money at all, she'd have had to pay $120 for a single album of the Stones.

Four years before her Munich triumph Olga knew what it was like to be one of the crowd. She lived in two small rooms with her invalid father, her three older sisters, and her mother, a dishwasher. It was only Olga's extraordinary talent for sports that had pulled her up from poverty.

But how can one compete in the Soviet Union without perfect aerial twists? Only 10 percent of the most outstanding Russian athletes remain in sports to become coaches or directors. The rest, with their sports careers ended, find themselves unable to adjust. Olympic weight-lifting champion Yuri Vlasov had to sell his car to support his wife and two children. European boxing champion Viktor Ageev, probably the most talented light-heavyweight ever to appear in Russia, sits in jail for street fighting. Two-time Olympic hockey champion Aleksandr Almetov died an alcoholic just two years after leaving the game.

While officially nonexistent, competition within Soviet society actually flourishes—in distorted form. Obtaining a good position in any field requires not only initiative, persistence, and intelligence but also expertise in the ancient Oriental art of maneuvering up a long staircase to the offices of the party bosses. At every step the athlete finds competitors who started the climb ten years earlier, while he or she was busy training. Those who once solicited the athlete to expend himself for the motherland, assuring him that she would never forsake him, now dismiss him with vague promises or proposals that he seek temporary work as a longshoreman or a hotel hairdresser. The winner loses out without a chance to play the game. Only a medal or an anecdote remains for the occasional entertainment of the neighbors.

Knowing this all too well, Olga persisted in sports. Yet, before the Montreal Olympics, she admitted, "I get scared. Sometimes I get goose bumps before going onto the platform. And the ankle I sprained at the World Cup in London still hurts." A few more injuries and she will no longer be able to compete.

Though Olga's performance on the beam in Montreal was clean and fast, it was hardly the dazzlingly unique routine she had rehearsed for four years. The judges frowned and gave her a 9.50. The Forum walls shook in the avalanche of boos that followed, and Latynina, in full view of the eighteen thousand spectators, rushed to the judges to protest. "They told me that Olga had been penalized for going over the time limit," she later explained. Olga added something about her ankle. Both of them knew the real story: "wooden legs."

Every gymnast on the Soviet team is taught by a physician to shut out the surroundings and concentrate fully on her routine, a preconditioning known as autogenics. When it succeeds, applause strikes the performer's ears like distant surf. Often a gymnast will look point-blank into the TV cameras and later ask his coach, "Why wasn't there any TV today?"

When one student of Soviet autogenics, after lying in a hospital for two years with broken vertebrae, finally had his bandages removed, the doctors expected to see a flabby body. They were stunned to see firm, bulging muscles. The patient explained that he had spent several hours a day at imaginary sports. Monday he ran 5,000 meters. Tuesday he pressed weights. Wednesday he wrestled in the gym.

Leonid Gissen, the Soviet Olympic Team psychologist, teaches athletes to relax by imagining feelings of warmth. "Let's pretend," he says, "that your arm is a large glass syringe. You feel as if it's pushing your blood down into your palms, into your fingers, and popping your skin. Your arm is burning." For purposes of concentration, he tells the athletes to imagine themselves under an ice-cold shower or the hairs on their arms freezing into stinging icicles. Liudmila Turishcheva, Gissen's best pupil, demonstrated the effectiveness of autogenics by springing almost three feet into the air from a prone position on an ordinary mattress.

A trained gymnast cuts out the audience with a mental curtain. Still, a message of former failure can break through this roadblock and reach the nerve centers. The gymnast suddenly zooms in on the face of a spectator in the fourteenth row. From that moment on, autogenics fades out and "wooden legs" takes over. The performer's mind is bombarded by the events around her, and her program falls into chaos. Seconds drag into minutes, lips become dry, and eyes blur with sweat. Legs, arms, head—everything injured in earlier falls begins to resound in the memory like bells, turning finally into an illusion of actual pain.

When this is the case, an experienced gymnast can summon the power to switch to an easier program to avoid falling. This had been Olga's choice. As though exchanging an evening gown for a housedress, Olga staved off the fear. But all hope for the gold was lost.

The floor exercise was next.

With baggy shirts and pants and wearing heavy boots more useful for puncturing permafrost than walking on asphalt, the Russian tourists at the Games were easy to identify. Their cheers were synchronized, as if they had come to the Forum solely to put the disorderly Westerners to shame with their organized camaraderie. In one section two dozen Russians rooted under the direction of a bilious gentleman with a shopping bag at his feet crammed with booty raided from Montreal department stores. Methodical and emotionless, he gave his commands for noise making like the foreman of a spike-pounding construction brigade on the Trans-Siberian railroad. Between orders he busied himself with the contents of the bag, smugly fingering his cornucopia of shorts and socks, pantyhose and brassieres. While his hands waved patriotically, his feet maintained contact with the bag, either for inspiration or out of fear that his neighbors might take an interest in it.

Perhaps the cheerleader really had worked in construction—had worked so hard that he had won the chance to travel. In fact, the whole cheering squad might just as easily have included a turner who had overfulfilled his gear-machining quota by 300 percent, a weaver who had tended twenty-four looms instead of the usual twelve, or a shepherd who had managed to drive simultaneously a flock of sheep, a herd of cows, and a pen of pigs.

Such workers are rewarded: after passing defection clearance they are dispatched around the world to see the Place de l'Opéra in Paris, the Doge's Palace in Venice, or the Olympic Games in Montreal. In most cases at Montreal, the Soviet government had paid the full $1,350 per person for a package tour to the Games. An additional $110 spending money was a substantial start toward picking up Western goods for profitable resale on Moscow's black market.

Unlike the Americans, who were waving stars and stripes everywhere the eye could see, the Russians came unarmed: the red flag of the USSR is regarded as a sacred banner, to be held aloft only when storming the fortresses of capitalism.

Moreover, whereas the Americans broke into a tearful "Oh, say can you see . . ." during the medals presentation, the Russians remained stonily silent when their own anthem was played. Their problem began thirty-five years ago, when the anthem was written. The main refrain starts with the words, "We were brought up by Stalin, who inspired us to be faithful to the people, to labor and heroic deeds . . ." In 1956 Nikita Khrushchev, busy erasing Stalin's name from cities, streets, ships, schools, and libraries, somehow overlooked the anthem. Now embarrassed to mention Stalin's name in public and anxiously wondering to whom they owed their upbringing, the Russians could only listen to the solemn copper cymbals of the band.

The Rusians also encountered a linguistic problem at the Forum, for the great treasury of the Russian language contains only two sports cheers: *Molodets!* (Atta boy!) and *Shaibu!* (Hockey puck!)—both clearly unsuitable for the occasion. In preference to silence, they manufactured creative new collective chants: "Olia! Olia" (Korbut), "Liuda! Liuda!" (Turishcheva) and "Nelia! Nelia!" (Kim), depending on which of the girls happened to be up.

During rest breaks the Russians traded badges, pens, notebooks, and ruble coins with the other fans, who seemed genuinely enthusiastic about real Soviet goods. One man, his exchange commodities exhausted, modestly proposed trading his Moscow-made wristwatch for his neighbor's Rolex. The deal fell through.

In a warm-up before the floor exercise, Olga rushed headlong into a double somersault with a twist. The crowd howled with delight, most without ever realizing she had pulled off a stunt that had never before been attempted —even in the real event. Half a minute later she again broke into a run, took off into flight, rotated until she peaked, and began to fall, face down, like a disoriented diver in a bellyflop. Latynina rushed out onto the platform. In the last instant Olga recovered and landed on her side, jumping to her feet as if nothing had happened. She ran into the corner and took her starting position—waiting, not moving, her body glowing waxlike, her eyes bulging, looking silently at Latynina. Olga was in trouble.

It was better to leave her alone. Latynina walked away, and for a third time Olga cut loose into a double somersault.

A gambler with her life at stake, Olga was no longer playing for the audience's love or victory over Liudmila and Nadia. After three events she already knew that she had lost to them. It was to herself she dared not lose.

Then began "In Memory of Edith Piaf," a musical étude written for Olga which signaled the start of the last event —the actual floor competition.

Olga danced the exercise as if finally cutting the knot of gravitation. She seemed to hover in midair. She landed on the floor, interpreting the words of the great French song-stress with hands, legs, shoulders, and eyes: "*Rien—je ne regrette rien.*"

She scored 9.85, but she no longer cared. A little later, without waiting for the end of the competition, she walked out of the arena.

In scoring vaulting, a balanced, motionless landing is as important as the vault itself. The gymnast is permitted just one step in the direction of the dismount. Mitsuko Tsukahara herself had rarely managed to stick.

When Nelli Kim planted herself firmly on the floor after spinning around her forward axis and parting the air like a tomahawk, the judges flashed a 10 without hesitation.

"How did she do it?" I asked her coach, Vladimir Baidin, a beefy, black-haired man with the weathered face of a truck driver who ferries fruits from the Caucasus to Moscow.

"Easy! With the help of science. Scientific training, the scientific analysis of jumps, the scientific education of Nelli," he answered confidently, sounding like a Russian translation of Muhammad Ali.

In order to study the ways of science, I watched Nelli's

next landing more closely. All I discovered was an appealing girl with Oriental eyes, dynamically arched brows, and a coltlike gallop—a gift, I guessed, from her ancestors, nomads of the wild steppes. If there was any hint of science, perhaps it was to be found hidden in her heels, in the form of retrorockets.

"I developed a fifty-point scale that measures a girl's chances of becoming an outstanding athlete," Baidin declared proudly.

"For example?"

"Distance from home to the gymnastics school. If it's more than a half-hour bus ride, forget it! Or, the best and most popular girl in the class—no way! Or, family tree. Nelli's mother's a Tartar and her father's Korean. In other words, she's an Asiatic. They're born gymnasts, like the Japanese—rugged, with a dry body and bones that bend like they're made of plastic. Or the Rumanians. They eat *mamalyga* all their lives. There's something in that corn mush that makes their girls weightless. Four years ago in Varna I saw Nadia Comaneci for the first time. I lifted her up. She felt like a speck of dust."

Baidin's explanation was interrupted by Latynina, who was nervously drifting toward him.

In 1971 I used to visit the Moscow House of Journalists regularly. The House of Journalists is a club—something like a "21" for the creative workers of Communism.

In an ordinary Moscow restaurant, waiters are concerned not with how to serve clients politely but with how to get rid of them as quickly as possible; their salaries depend on the number of diners they process per day. In the journalist's club you can sit as long as your soul desires—and the Russian soul is almost boundless, if there's vodka and beer around. Tables are slammed together, strangers become friends, and everyone is agreed on dishing the Kremlin— elsewhere a rarely permissible conversational delicacy.

On several occasions I happened to be at the club at the same time as Larisa Latynina and her husband, Viktor Mikhailov, a soft-spoken blond-haired man with lackluster eyes who wore a gray suit—in a word, the personification of Russian unobtrusiveness. In accomplishment, however, Mikhailov was rather more conspicuous: the head of the Team Sports Department of the Sports Committee of the USSR. I was astounded to learn later that he had been arrested and sentenced to death for running a criminal syndicate that had raked in hundreds of thousands of rubles.

Day and night, Moscow's single auto showroom is besieged by crowds of bleary-eyed citizens, often southerners armed with stained suitcases and dirty duffel bags. The ancient dust of the narrow trails of the Caucasus covers their horsemen's boots, but these citizens are looking for neither leather saddles nor bridles and horseshoes. They want a car, be it an M-24 Volga sedan or an old Dodge Polara, for which they'll shell out $25,000—double the official price. And they can pay: their suitcases and bags are crammed with the loot of the illegal businesses that flourish throughout the southern republics of the USSR—everything from dealing hashish to the moonlight manufacturing of fake furs.

Via a ring of middlemen, car lovers were introduced to the "big boss," Mikhailov, who would make them happy for a reasonable bribe. It happened that a business associate of Mikhailov's was Marshal Semën Budënnyi, a legendary hero of the Revolution and chairman of the Soviet Federation of Equestrian Sports and Thoroughbred

Racing. A prospective customer, ready with two packets of money, would be invited into Mikhailov's limousine— one of the packets for the car, and the other for the bribe. The gentlemen would then drive to the Army Sports Club's race track, where Budënnyi's residence was located.

The marshal's office was walled in with bulletproof glass, so that from the limousine the customer could clearly see Mikhailov enter the office, shake hands with the marshal, and sit down to talk—for an hour, an hour and a half. The marshal would then sign some papers, among which, the customer assumed, was his application for a car from the warehouse reserved for supplying outstanding sportsmen. Mikhailov would then return to the limousine, give his customer a pat on the back, and hand him his application with the marshal's approval. "Step on it!" Mikhailov would order jocularly, pocketing the bribe.

Halfway to the warehouse the limousine would be stopped by a squad of plainclothesmen, who would arrest both the briber and the bribed and confiscate the car money. If the comrade from the south could come up with another bribe in the next few days, this time for the police, he was set free.

It was a reliable old con game, Soviet-style, in which Mikhailov would be released forthwith by his gang of cop cronies. The working assumption of the game was that the briber would never talk, unless he was willing to be locked up in Siberia for a decade. So the business rolled on lucratively for several years, the loot divided among the Mikhailov gang while the innocent Budënnyi signed papers for the relocation of Arabian geldings across Russia.

Co-leader of the gang was Anatolii Ruslov, a Moscow police captain, who decided not to miss out on a good thing and made Mikhailov his partner. The two were finally

trapped after swindling one of the underground millionaires. It happened that the KGB, which operates separately
from the police, eventually arrested the millionaire for
reasons of their own. The first thing he told was a fascinating tale about a police captain and a sports executive.

Sentences are usually meted out in the USSR according
to the amount of money an individual possesses: if Socialist
laws were applied in the United States, most millionaires
would be lined up before a firing squad. Mikhailov's personal take must have come to less than a million, because
he was punished with a prison sentence instead of a bullet.
Later he was pardoned.

No matter what Mikhailov had done, he remained
Latynina's husband and the father of her child. She
waited for him for five years. This in itself may have all
been well and good, but when one is a senior coach of the
Soviet National Team such devotion is considered a liability; when Latynina heatedly defended Olga at the
Forum, the judges looked at her with surprise and dismay.
She had spent at least half a dozen of her twenty-five years
in gymnastics as a judge at international competitions.
Like them, she knew the difficulty and responsibility of
calculating the results of years of painstaking work in just
a few moments. Like every one of the judges at the Forum,
she knew the words of Arthur Gander: "Only a gymnast
who makes the judges drop their pencils is worth more
than a 9.50." And, like all of them, she knew Olga's performance had fallen short.

Wending her way past the judges' tables and appealing
dramatically to the officials, Latynina was attempting to
convince not the people present but those on Skatertnaia
Street in Moscow that she still deserved to head the Soviet

team despite two failures: love for a convict and inability to present a Russian Comaneci.

The next day, when the gymnastics competition was over, I interviewed Nelli Kim. Our conversation took place in a packed car of the Montreal metro. I sat between Nelli and Baidin.

We had met that morning in front of the Olympic Village. Nelli had let down her black hair and was wearing jeans and a maroon shirt, the tails tied above her midriff. "I have no time now," she said. "We're going into town. If you like, we can talk on the way." Then she yawned so sweetly that all my questions derailed in a flash. Looking closely at her, I asked, "How come your eyes are red?"

"The other girls and I didn't go to bed until five in the morning."

"The other girls" were Olga and Liudmila. For the first time after their long battle they had had a chance to take it easy—beginning with the Olympic Village discotheque; continuing at 2 A.M. in the cafeteria, where they stuffed themselves on cake, salad, ice cream, mashed potatoes, and beef Stroganoff; and ending at the swimming pool, where they greeted the sunrise and shared their plans for the weeks to come.

"I'm going to go out to the country for horses—real, not wooden—with grass and clover."

"How about your great homecoming celebration in Chimkent?" I asked.

"They're too busy pushing the grain harvest. They're not in the mood for gymnastics."

Baidin hastened to correct her. "A conference will be obligatory."

The day before had been her happiest ever, she told me. The unhappy ones were those she spent training in the gym.

"Why?" I asked. "Fear?"

"Among other things. And the fear is different for each apparatus. For example, before vaulting I'm only afraid when I'm running toward the horse, but as soon as I touch it and take off into the air, I'm not a human anymore, I'm a computer."

"Do you think that Comaneci or Olga or Liudmila can't do a full-twisting Tsukahara?" Baidin interjected. "Of course they can—landing on their nose, on their side, their hands. But only Nelli can land standing, her feet dug into the floor."

Nelli became livelier. She described her tricks, gesticulating excitedly. Baidin drew a sketch: "This jump's eighty percent Nelli, fifteen percent me, and five percent Dr. Antonov."

A Japanese recognized Nelli and asked to take a picture. He snapped without looking into the viewfinder.

"Glory?" Nelli continued. "It's my engine and ambition —maybe the main thing that keeps me going. I compete with the girls, and if I see they're going better . . . well, I think to myself, I'll show them!" Lips compressed, mouth distorted, eyes lit up—yes, a descendant of the wild nomads.

"I'm only mad on the platform. I want myself to be violent: otherwise I wouldn't be competitive. But as soon as it's over, that vanishes." Nelli giggled slyly and primped her hair, obviously aware that by now there were three Japanese clicking Nikons.

"I feel sorry for Olga—we're roommates at the Olympic

Village, you know. I'm the one that's happy now, and she's suffering day and night. That's the curse of sports. Somebody's got to lose."

Two days earlier Baidin had told me: "As a gymnast I was only mediocre. I never even made it to the USSR championships. Yet I always wanted to achieve something great, so I put my search for greatness into Nelli, once I found her. She was nine: skinny, shoulder blades sharp enough to cut yourself on, bandy-legged. It took ten years to make her and prove you don't have to be an outstanding athlete to be a coach.

"If your girl fails, you don't go around bragging about your project. You'd be ridiculed. Not only that: you'd be relieved of your job. And nobody knows about your sleepless nights and the nitroglycerin tablets in your pockets. Now Nelli's hot: Moscow, Leningrad, and Kiev have invited her, promising her a chic life. You can bet it's not like in our hick town, Chimkent. Maybe she'll go; that would hurt. What am I without her? But you can't cage a bird like her. Well, anyway, I've got other pupils, and all I want is for them to come into the gym ten, twenty years from now, like into a church, get absolution for their sins. Gymnastics is a religion, primordial and pure."

Observing the vivacious girl tapping her worn-out sneakers on the floor of the subway car, I wonder how long she'd last in the nunnery of gymnastics with neither Liudmila's fanatic dedication nor Olga's thirst for discovery.

"What do you think of your coach?"

"He's like a second father," she said as a matter of course. "He used to let boys come to my house for Saturday night dance parties. We called them 'calisthenic evenings,' part of the training process." She smiled. "My mother said,

'If it's O.K. with Vladimir Borisovich, it's O.K. with me.' Even when I have problems with my friends, the one in Bulgaria or the one in Alma-Ata, I let the coach decide."

Nelli noticed the Montreal *Gazette* in my hands and caught the front-page headline: "Nelli Kim, Nadia Share Gymnastic Glory."

"My God," she exclaimed in horror as she read on. "Twenty-one! They're crazy!" The article had misstated her age.

"You're nineteen." Baidin comforted her. "And the only nineteen-year-old Honored Master of Sport in the USSR."

While we talked, Nelli's new fame threatened to end our talk. Bodies surged toward her menacingly. The Japanese camera clickers were supplanted by Germans, all of them outnumbered by arms waving for autographs. Nelli signed them mechanically while Baidin and I formed a flying wedge.

After a harrowing escape onto the platform we managed to find a coffee shop where we could talk a little longer. I wanted to know her plans for the future.

"To study English really hard."

Nelli was looking forward to an exhibition tour around the United States, but her main interest in English was to plumb the mysteries of American horror movies.

"How much of the tour's profit will go to the Soviet government?" I asked.

Calmly scratching her head like an experienced book-keeper, she answered, "A million." I told her that in the United States many performers can get a million for themselves alone, if they're popular, and that gymnastics is not without an audience. My information aroused a respectful reaction and the comment, "No kidding!" But Coach

Baidin was on the alert: "We don't need money. We have everything we need."

We parted in front of Eaton's department store. Baidin and Nelli went in to buy a tape deck for her car—the last detail necessary for the happiness of a triple gold medal winner.

FOUR

The Russian Pelé and Soviet Soccer

For many Russian fans, the personification of their 1956 Olympic soccer triumph was center forward Eduard Streltsov.

Olympic rules state clearly that only players who've been in a final game are awarded a medal. Streltsov hadn't. "You can't handle the tension," his trainer had inexplicably insisted. The nineteen-year-old crowd-throb with the uncanny knack of scoring in the most hopeless of situations trudged back to the bench and kicked the hell out of the air while his team got ripped to shreds. It was only by a miracle that at the last minute the Russians stole the game from Yugoslavia without him. The gold was given to his substitute, Nikita Simonian, who headed for Streltsov the moment the ceremony was over.

"Take the medal, Edik. You carried us all the way, and you're the one that deserves it." It goes without saying that Streltsov declined, but the nobility of the exchange quickly joined the legends surrounding the player.

Every country longs to have a hero. In America heroes

surface more or less spontaneously, but their emergence in Russia is planned by the propaganda section of the Central Committee of the Communist Party. By order of party potentates, eminent workers of every walk of life are launched into prominence by television. These exemplars of socialism often turn out to be semiliterates who find making a minor speech as distressing as undergoing public execution. The masses are ready enough to sympathize with the anxiety of the media-hyped heroes but slower to emulate their valiant feats of labor.

Passionate illusions are born unprompted on the soccer field, though, where simple ballplayers are transformed into public personalities. Since quality athletes clearly aren't packaged in a Kremlin office, they suggest a subtle flavor of freedom and self-determination. Muscular and clean-cut, they exude universal appeal. Streltsov was that kind of personality.

It may be that Russians can endure empty food stores, communal bathrooms, and the terror of the secret police, but injustice done to a soccer hero can send an army of citizens to the barricades. On his return to Moscow from Melbourne, Streltsov was named an Honored Master of Sport and awarded the Order of the Red Banner—the highest civilian decoration after the Order of Lenin. Two years later the following note, entitled "In the Halls of Justice," appeared in *Pravda*: "The former soccer player E. Streltsov has been sentenced to eight years in a correctional labor camp."

Once I was watching as Streltsov received a pass from the touchline. The ball sailed toward him at chest level. A fellow forward was standing to his left, with a pair of opposing fullbacks waiting in front and the goalie behind them. There were two logical possibilities: either to stop the ball with his gut, let it drop to his feet, and attack the backs, or pass the ball to his teammate on the left. Streltsov's opponents watched him closely. He was motionless; only his eyes were alive. But in the pause he had given himself a chance to study the goalie—the tilt of his head, the inclination of his body, the position of his feet. Streltsov saw the goalie's right leg straighten slightly, as if readying for a jolt: he'd defend the left corner, believing that Streltsov, blocked by two fullbacks, would pass the ball to his teammate. In fact, Streltsov moved back as if to make way for the approaching ball. The goalie and now both backs turned their attention to the left inside and shifted their bodies accordingly. With lightning speed, Streltsov rushed forward and, dipping, headed the ball into the right corner.

Usually, however, the attack of the 6'2", 195-pound Streltsov resembled the crushing movement of a tank, scattering opponents along the way like toy soldiers. His kick carried a force of a good 2,500 pounds. On one occasion a ball he booted actually broke through the net from the outside, an inch from the upright, and the referee called the point. Though it may have been the deciding game of the European championship, Streltsov jogged up to the judge to call the mistake.

The player's passes were so precise that one would have sworn the ball had eyes. He devised a mid-attack backward pass with his heel to a partner who'd shoot at the defenseless goal. It seemed as though nothing was impossible for him.

Sports commentators have written ecstatically about the "dry leaf"—the famous corner kick of the Brazilian Didi.

Didi would place the ball in the corner of the field and arrange it endlessly. Starting practically at the stands, he'd run up to the ball and kick so that it sailed straight ahead and suddenly change direction for the goal. The maneuver required mathematically precise technique.

Streltsov had seen the "dry leaf" only once when the Soviet team got a shot at the corner in the second half of a game with Brazil. He kicked quickly, without preparation. The ball soared and, tracking a fantastic curlicue, spun into the goal.

Soccer experts compare Streltsov to Pelé. But unlike the Brazilian, the Russian failed to exploit even half his talent.

In the fall of 1957 the players of the National Team gathered at Moscow's Belorusskii Station to leave for a game against Poland that would decide the finalist for the '58 world championships in Sweden. Streltsov and his friend Valentin Ivanov failed to show.

Most athletes are superstitious, and Russian soccer players are no exception. They'll play in their beat-up but "lucky" soccer shoes for years, they'll grab the same lucky seats in the bus, train, or plane on the way to the game, and they'll just about quit the field if they don't see their lucky reporter behind the gate. Since outright superstitiousness is frowned upon under the materialist philosophy of Marxism, coaches prefer a euphemism for the embarrassing backsliding: psychological preparation.

Streltsov's and Ivanov's psychological preparation before any away game consisted of a champagne dinner in a restaurant in Sokolniki Park. The day they should have appeared at Belorusskii, there were just too many other diners approaching with glasses raised to wish them luck.

To a Russian, not to drink up on a toast is a sure sign of bad luck. To make a long story short, by the time the two friends arrived at the station the team train had left.

The first to sober up was Streltsov, who charged through the precinct door at the station. The soccer king's pull seemed boundless. In no time the streets of Moscow were filled with the scream of sirens as a motorized cortege went in hot pursuit of the express. The cars caught up with the train at Mozhaisk, a local stop 26 miles out of Moscow. Although an international express is not allowed to stop there under any circumstances, it only took a couple of words from the forward for the local official to send up his red signal. In a matter of seconds Streltsov and Ivanov were standing before the livid senior coach, Gavriil Kachalin, who had already phoned the Sports Committee about the disappearance of the pair. The sports bureaucracy spent two days digesting the question of whether to allow the offenders on the field or to keep them under house arrest. The day of the match the coach received the following telegram: LET PLAY. WILL INVESTIGATE ON RETURN, DEPENDING ON GAME. To translate: Score, or be expelled from the team.

Minutes after kickoff, Streltsov collided in midair with the back guarding him and dropped, unconscious, to the turf. Coming to, he tried to stand up and couldn't. He crawled onto the track, overwhelmed with the pain of a pulled hamstring but imploring the team doctor to send him back in. The doctor applied ice to the leg and wrapped it in an elastic bandage. Streltsov scored the winning goal.

Two months after the game the players were given time off for winter vacation. On January 29, 1958, Streltsov got soused in the Sovetskii Restaurant, became involved in a brawl, and ended up in the nearest police station. (Massive free-for-alls in Russian restaurants are something of a tradition, dating back to the time of Ivan the Terrible, when a man's worth was defined by his ability to bloody another.) Naturally, the forward was kept comfortably apart from the other, less distinguished, offending parties, put in a well-appointed limousine, and quietly escorted home.

In Moscow, where word of mouth spreads faster than wire services, an incident involving an athlete of Streltsov's stature can't be hushed up for long. By the next day all of Moscow was savoring tidbits telling how Streltsov's right leg had sent one assailant flying up to the chandeliers while his left had smashed through a brick wall.

On February 2 *Komsomolskaia Pravda* delivered the player a blow by publishing an article trenchantly entitled "Starstruck"—a signal that initiated an avalanche of attack to follow. On February 4, at a meeting of the National Team, the goalie, Communist Lev Yashin, announced, "This has gone too far. It's time to drive the black sheep out of the flock." On February 5 the Sports Committee resolved to take Streltsov off the team roster and rescind his Honored Master of Sport.

Soccer fans panicked. Even had they been convinced that their idol was the villainous fiend the newspapers made him out to be, they knew too well that without him the team didn't stand a chance in the upcoming championships in Sweden. Tens of thousands of letters and telegrams, from individual comrades and huge collectives, mines and factories, schools and institutes, bombarded the Kremlin to demand that the hero be pardoned. The Streltsov affair had become an open national controversy.

On April 16 *Komsomolskaia Pravda* published the following letter from Streltsov: "I am deeply aware of my deplorable behavior, criticized quite justly in the article 'Starstruck.' I promise to mend my ways and devote everything in my power to prove worthy of the lofty distinction of Soviet Sportsman." In the Aesopian language of the Russian press, the publication of the letter signified that the masses had won the issue.

Streltsov played a stunning game against England on May 23. Millions sighed with relief to know that the once unimaginable—a Soviet World Cup victory—was again a real possibility.

Having sized up the Russian Tank, the manager of a wealthy West German club approached Streltsov with an offer for after Sweden. The manager wasn't so naïve as to negotiate with the Sports Committee, knowing full well that they'd never agree to trade their best player to the odious West. The alternative was to solicit his defection in Stockholm.

Streltsov stayed noncommittal but confided the flattering proposition to a teammate. The figure loomed before him seductively: $250,000 for a single year! With lots of travel already under his belt, he had no trouble picturing the things he could buy with a stash like that. In a land of comprehensive surveillance this kind of offer inevitably reaches the ears of the authorities. The question of whether a troublemaker like Streltsov could be trusted arose once again in the Sports Committee.

An answer was startlingly prompt in forthcoming. Streltsov was arrested a week before Sweden and charged with rape. The victim was examined and evidence collected. The girl in the case was the daughter of an army general and World War II hero.

. . .

The players leave the locker room at Luzhniki Stadium through a tunnel to the service exit, where a bevy of wives and girlfriends awaits them after every game. The women all know one another. Only Streltsov's girls were strangers, there being a new one almost every game. His personal appearance at private Moscow theater clubs and film screenings created minor fracases among the models and actresses, who'd lose interest in their dates on the spot. At twenty-one, Streltsov was Moscow's most eligible bachelor: in addition to his legendary legs, he boasted a high forehead, thick blond hair, blue eyes, and a strong jaw.

After the political thaw in the late fifties, the youth of Moscow and Leningrad became infatuated with America. The more fashionable of the young men began calling themselves stateniks; while they may have had trouble getting hold of American clothes, they did learn to tell Basie from Brubeck. Only a few—Streltsov among them—were in a position to parade in Brooks Brothers suits and Bostonian boots. Claiming to be sexually liberated, the girls that would hang out with the stateniks often became the object of newspaper attacks branding them common whores. Media hysteria notwithstanding, none of them took money for their company: the fact was that they were never in financial need, all being members of the elite—mere rebels against the boredom of Soviet socialism.

The evening of the arrest, a group of stateniks was lured by the name of Streltsov to a small-scale saturnalia being thrown by the players at the five-room apartment of Boris Tatushin, the right inside of the National Team. After a number of drinks and sexual encounters under wall posters proclaiming "Communism Is Hard but Inspiring Work," the guests were invited to change partners.

The famous general's attractive daughter was no new-comer to these gatherings. A psychology student at Moscow University, her nocturnal debauches seemed less the evidence of passion than a preoccupation with researching human sexual behavior. Catching sight of Streltsov, she seemed instantly transformed, convinced that she had happened at last upon the man of her life.

Having heard of the fate of Streltsov's other one-night stands, girls he had virtually forgotten by morning, the general's daughter, still the cold-blooded analyst, devised a plan of subjugation—Soviet in form but Asian in essence: to ply him with vodka until his brain shut down (hardly the greatest obstacle) and, after intercourse, to cry rape, scratching herself to provide evidence and fighting him to attract witnesses—tenants from every floor of a building full of Moscow VIPs.

Yuri Shalamov, a sports photographer for *Komsomolskaia Pravda* at the time, had firsthand access to the police report: "At first we were astounded. It seemed unbelievable. Why would Streltsov have to use force when literally every girl in Moscow would have considered herself lucky to spend the night with him? Later we discovered that this one was counting on his reputation for indiscretions under the influence and concluded that her rape story would be not only credible but easy to prove. Soviet laws would do the rest."

The criminal code of the USSR provides that if a rape victim agrees to withdraw her accusation the court will drop the affair. An out-of-court settlement usually has just one condition: instant marriage. But the Streltsov case began moving in a direction the girl couldn't have predicted.

Streltsov was needed desperately for the prestige of

Soviet sports. But the Sports Committee officials knew that hushing up the scandal, even temporarily, would be difficult. What was worse, they had lost all hope that he could be trusted; now they seriously began fearing that he might defect. Would it be worth interceding for him only to have so much greater embarrassment in the future?

Meanwhile, rumors rolled in concentric waves to the most distant corners of the country, by which point fishermen in Vladivostok were convinced that Streltsov had wounded a dozen cops with a Kalashnikov in a desperate shoot-out at the time of arrest. The letters to the editor that began inundating the newspapers suggested that the forward be taken in an armored car to Stockholm to score and rushed back to Moscow for a trial afterward.

In the meantime, the girl's father, shocked by his daughter's scratches and bruises, stormed police headquarters with his personal pistol and threatened to blow Streltsov's brains out if he was released. It was hard not to take the former division commander at Stalingrad seriously. The general bemoaned his besmirched honor, threatening at one point to kill his own daughter if she dared plead leniency for the culprit. The case had clearly gotten out of hand.

The omnipotent sports fans of the Central Committee of the Communist Party were confronted with a serious dilemma. To free the forward meant setting a precedent by which sports stars, who already enjoyed the highest standard of living and the most generous privileges in the nation, would be able to do whatever they pleased: to drink unrestrainedly, fight freely, rape, plunder, and shed innocent blood. The "power of example," the cornerstone of Communist propaganda, would backfire to destroy Soviet sports.

It was concluded that guilty or not guilty, Streltsov would better serve the cause of Communism if stashed away in Siberia. Like all cases of such extreme importance, the matter was brought to the attention of Nikita Khrushchev for the final word.

A cursory examination of Luzhniki Stadium reveals a booth with a concrete top and bulletproof glass walls lost among the stands like a bomb shelter and designed for the sports fans in the Politburo. The booth is surrounded by open stands holding an additional two hundred ministers, diplomats, and journalists. Lev Mozhaev, chief engineer of the stadium before emigrating to the United States in 1975, has described it:

> The Politburo bunker at Luzhniki is carpeted in red, wall to wall. It has a bar that stocks whiskey, scotch, vodka, cognac, caviar, and American cigarettes. In addition, there's a short-wave apparatus. The bunker is guarded year round; even though I was an executive of the stadium, I had to fight to get in just once a year, in April, to begin regular repairs and set it up for the arrival of the Politburo members for the annual sports holiday on the second of May.
>
> The bunker's staff, made up of a manager, bartenders, waitresses, janitors, and doormen, was salaried off the books and outside of stadium jurisdiction. Everyone on the staff was a member of the party who had also graduated from the "service" curriculum of the secret-police academy and been assigned to Section Nine of the KGB, which handles the protection of Politburo bosses at public events.
>
> Given the fact that Luzhniki [the main arena for the 1980 Olympics] has seating for 107,000 less than angelic spectators, the reinforced-concrete ceilings of the bunker undergoes heavy overloads, and I could never dismiss the possibility of a cave-in.

The day before the arrival of the Politburo, Section Nine sent three regiments of soldiers to the stadium. This army was concentrated around the government stands and ordered to imitate the crowds by marching, jumping, stamping, shouting, and brawling for two hours nonstop. This accomplished, the officials of the stadium and Section Nine went into the bunker, checked for cracks along every inch of the walls and floors, and went out again, leaving security agents behind to stand guard until the Politburo's arrival.

The persons for whom the red-carpeted bunker was built have had a variety of attitudes toward soccer.

Stalin was never inside the stadium, limiting his contact with athletes to standing above the Lenin mausoleum and waving his hand perfunctorily at parades. For entertainment, the Best Friend of the People preferred foreign spy and gangster films.

Stalin's son Vasilii, on the other hand, was a soccer addict. When in September 1952 the Soviets lost to Yugoslavia at the Helsinki Olympics, the team of the Central Army Club (the basis for the National Team) was dissolved and certain of its members and their trainer, Boris Arkadev, interrogated by the KGB as suspected agents of Tito. Seizing the moment, Vasilii, then a lieutenant general of the Air Force and commander of the Moscow garrison, formed an Air Force club, sparing some of the better players the terror of Beria. The club lasted for two years—exactly until Vasilii himself, in the aftermath of his father's death, was discharged from all posts and stripped of his title.

Nikita Khrushchev visited Luzhniki only for Soviet-American track meets. At a party conference not long after one of these meets, Khrushchev, ever obsessed with overtaking the United States in agricultural and industrial production and never quite achieving the desired results, shook his fists and shouted, "Brumel really showed those mothers!"

Leonid Brezhnev is drawn equally to soccer and hockey. In 1973, when the players of the Central Army hockey club refused to work with coach Anatolii Tarasov on grounds of "pedagogical sadism," the leaders of the Sports Committee refrained from removing him without Brezhnev's personal sanction. The General Secretary gave his approval but two years later recommended Tarasov as trainer to the Central Army soccer team.

Many sports executives and journalists believe that if Brezhnev had had any decision-making power in 1958 he would have dealt with the Streltsov case more liberally. But Khrushchev was boss at the time and, in the heat of the anti-Stalinist campaign, was obliged to insist on the restoration of "Socialist law" and "genuine justice." In addition, he had been political commissar at Stalingrad and identified with what the general had gone through. His answer was to let the procurator's office decide. In other words, Streltsov was ordered behind bars.

DRINKING IS A RELIC OF THE PAST. ALCOHOLISM IS A CONGENITAL BLEMISH OF CAPITALISM. The slogans accompanied Russians at work, on the street, and at home. The newspapers and the radio, party organizers and public lecturers, called for diminished liquor consumption and frightened the populace with talk of cirrhotic livers, collapsed kidneys, and boggled brains. Tearful housewives told TV audiences tragic stories of how their lives had been ruined by drinking husbands. Yet sixty years after the Revolution, the Soviet Union remains blanketed with "blemishes" and awash with "relics."

YURI SHALAMOV

YURI SHALAMOV

    Liudmila Turishcheva reminded one of the noblewomen of Tolstoi or Turgenev—in leotards instead of crinoline . . . Vladislav "Iron Jaw" Rastorotskii spent years working to create a gymnastic machine out of a girl. He succeeded. But in the Montreal Olympics the human automaton finally cracked.

"I'm mad only on the platform," said Nelli Kim, triple gold-medal winner at the Montreal Olympics. "I want myself to be violent. Otherwise, I wouldn't be competitive. But as soon as it's over, that feeling vanishes."

Olga Korbut foisted an alien concept into Soviet philosophy: personality.

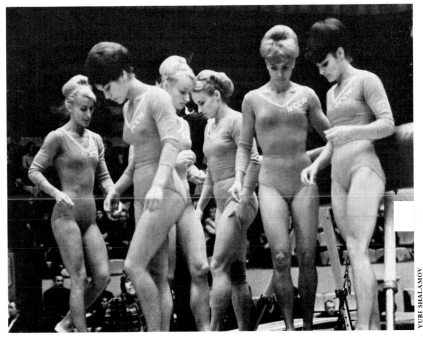

Coach of the Soviet Olympic Team, Larisa Latynina (second from right). In the current stampede to athleticism she declared that supercomplicated tricks means the inevitable disappearance of femininity in women's gymnastics.

To the future Korbuts now sweating in Russian gyms, sports offer a rare chance to make the leap from poverty to elite life.

LEV AND SASHA BORODULIN

Long-distance runner, Olympic champion in Melbourne, Vladimir Kuts. American sportswriter Arthur Daley said: "If Kuts has to kill himself to kill off the opposition, he has enough suicidal dedication to run himself to death." His words literally came true...

... At the age of twenty-nine, doctors informed Kuts that he could never run again. Eventually, after gaining 230 pounds, he died of a heart attack.

Valerii Brumel and John Thomas conducted a four-year athletic battle that involved psychological gimmicks, broken legs, politics, friendship, a lot of flowers, and six world records.

YURI SHALAMOV

Pentathlon star Irina Press. She and her sister Tamara won gold medals at Tokyo, but tongues wagged about their boyish appearance. When the International Olympic Committee began to check the sex of athletes in the games, Soviet track and field authorities quietly withdrew the sisters.

Soviet sports strategists did not expect great feats from sprinter Valerii Borzov because his training methods flew in the face of all their hallowed standards. But after Borzov's triumphs at Munich they were ready to put the sprinter and his coach in the pantheon of scientific geniuses.

The performance of Irina Rodnina and Aleksandr Zaitsev improved considerably when it was synchronized by a full-blown romance. The two became European, World, and Olympic champions—and husband and wife.

In Russia, passionate illusions are born unprompted on the soccer field, where simple ballplayers are transformed inevitably into public personalities.

YURI SHALAMOV

Although Russians have unlimited license to clobber the Canadians and the Swedes, they have to suffer bloody noses and slashed foreheads from the Czechs because of strict orders to keep "socialist comradeship" intact.

YURI SHALAMOV

Every spring, like robins at a worm sale, Moscow boys in full gear line up for as long as two miles outside the Central Army Club sports complex. Inside, Tarasov and team members hold tryouts, watching the young knights in armor demonstrate skating skill and shooting power.

Arkadii Chernyshëv, nominal coach, and Anatolii Tarasov, actual boss of the Soviet hockey squad. Uniquely uncompromising, Tarasov permitted neither party higher-ups nor sports commissars to tamper with his strategies or meddle with his rosters.

Nikita Khrushchev and Leonid Brezhnev with the Soviet Olympic champions. "Beat the hell out of the capitalists!"

That's weight-lifting life.

Vasilii Alekseev, now the strongest man in the world—but did steroids really help?

Leonid Zhabotinskii was preoccupied with perpetuating his Olympic crown into eternity. It lasted eight years.

YURI SHA

Yuri Vlasov was the first Russian superheavyweight to beat the record of Paul Anderson. The Soviet flag bearer at the Rome Olympics, he was in fact a most atypical representative of the Komsomol faithfuls, unwilling to obey Lenin's ethics of collectivism with anything short of sober, personal consideration.

Russians drink early in the morning and late at night, sitting behind kitchen tables and standing in dark doorways, from glasses and from the bottle. A bottle serves as a gift to a friend, a kickback to a business contact, a bribe to a policeman, or a token of appreciation to a plumber or repairman. In a land of strict gun control, it serves as the weapon of choice for drinkers of the more militant variety. If the glass of a bottle so used withstands contact with the human skull, it's delivered to a recycling center for a 25-cent return. A dozen empties buy a full.

Westerners think of all Russians as vodka drinkers. In fact, however, a bottle's content is a class marker. Stolichnaia vodka, with five medals on the label, and Armenian cognac, with five stars, are both unavailable at regular stores. These are the preserve of the Politburo and government, ministry executives and party functionaries, military officers and upper-echelon performers, all of whom drink at home and, in moods of respect for tradition, fling their glasses against a wall.

The middle class—engineeers, architects, junior executives, doctors, teachers, writers, and artists—drinks a port nicknamed "parfait." Members of the group run into each other after work in special stores that sell nothing but wines, mineral water, and fruits. The fruits are of poor quality and of interest to no one, and the mineral water is used only when observing the custom of drinking in threes, to rinse the glass brought along by one of the trio to knock off a parfait at the checkout counter.

Drinking in threes actually stems less from tradition than from economic necessity. Often the three are strangers, but with a common bond of limited resources and unlimited thirst, elaborate introductions are superfluous. Putting together $1.80 for a gargantuan bottle (60 cents a head), each drinks his share of the sweet Moldavian vintage. Nudged periodically by the elbows of his fellows, the wine running down his coat, he finishes off the remnants of the tobacco-sprinkled caramel in his trouser pocket and hastens home.

This arrangement is the most popular for the small-time intelligentsia; Moscow has few Western-type bars, and only foreigners, athletes, and black marketeers can afford them.

The working classes drink everywhere. On weekdays their preference is for Solntsedar ("V-2"), a wine that sells for $1.30 a liter. On weekends, in the heat of summer or the snows of winter, they line up in front of Blue Danubes, rickety light-blue sheds where they can get a mug of beer pumped from huge wooden kegs. Putting himself at a comfortable distance from the others, each man pulls a small bottle of rotgut out of his pants, pours the stuff into the mug of beer, and stirs the two with his index finger into a cocktail called an aurora borealis. Once the drink has loosened them up, the men drift into small groups and start in weighing the Dynamos' odds against the Torpedoes.

The peasants—one hundred million of them—find it too expensive to get really blotto on any of the state-produced liquors. Instead, they busy themselves between harvests distilling beets, grain, or sawdust into Samogon, a 150-proof home-brew that looks like watered-down milk.

Drunks make up a classless but rather broad category of the citizenry. These *alkashi* collect at grocery liquor departments—there are no separate liquor stores in the Soviet Union—by 11 A.M. *Alkashi*, who all seem to know one another, have but one concern: coming up with the three rubles, seventeen kopecks that'll buy a bottle of Moskovskaia, a cheap fluid that masquerades as vodka for the masses. Somehow they scrape up the money by noon and start in. By evening, once the Moskovskaia's gone, they're ready to drink anything—perfumes, lotions, varnishes, or stains. Pieces of cotton inserted into the cans of stain soak up the dye; what remains is a pale yellow chemical they mix with seltzer.

The day of a big soccer game class differences fade away. A goal for the home team will have a factory director kissing the locomotive machinist next to him and an army colonel embracing the cabbie down the bench.

Watching twenty-two athletes run and jump around a field has become a necessity for millions—a spectacle in which to lose themselves, a chance to live through the birth and sudden death of maneuvers. Every man fancies himself a coach, a strategist mapping imaginative attacks. The game is a chance to gamble, to take risks; a safety valve for his savagery; a time to forget the hardships and futility of his life. This kind of concentrated drama can't be handled by a Russian without a bottle, a fact that has turned Soviet stadiums into saloons under the sky.

By the end of a game, Luzhniki takes on the look of a giant bottle warehouse. A chain of men and women was once illegally organized to carry the empty bottles out of the stadium in potato sacks, load them into trucks, and transport them to the collection centers. The monthly profits of the members equaled the salary of the head of a state ministry.

Too busy with monitoring the drunks, the authorities used to look the other way. But when ten thousand temperamental Georgians began a melee at a game in the late sixties between Moscow's Spartak and the Tbilisi Dynamos that was barely suppressed by the regular troops of the Moscow garrison and ended in the death of several men, it was ordered that no one be admitted carrying shopping bags or briefcases, the presumed means of bagging in the booze. Like airport security agents, stadium employees and volunteer police were stationed at all entrances to scan the fans. Every bottle found was confiscated on the spot and thrown into an enormous metal drum.

Enterprising fans reacted by downing the contents of their bottles outside the stadium fences and going in as smashed as ever. The government's response, in turn, was the sobering station. Shabby, unheated, 100-bed barracks with efficient cold showers were set up near every precinct station in all twenty-nine boroughs of Moscow.

The day of a game, police buses barricade the stadium. As events on the field start heating up, the buses start filling up. At the sobering station the raging drunks are examined by doctors for injuries. If the clients fail to cooperate in undressing or seem reluctant to enjoy the cold shower, they're introduced to karate; the injuries sustained by these soccer fans in the stands are only the beginning of their sorrows. Once beaten, a fan tends to quiet down on his bed, his legs and hands tied to iron pintles and his naked back marked with large ink numbers for identification.

The next morning, with a $25 ticket in his pocket and a letter describing his deplorable deportment on its way to his place of work, the fan departs for his lathe, his drawing board, or his desk—a quiet and hardworking citizen once again.

For all his outstanding talent, Eduard Streltsov was not a man to defy tradition, and at the age of fourteen the apprentice metalworker was introduced to a Russian custom whereby the young worker wets his senior's whistle on payday. What distinguished Streltsov was his passion for the soccer field, and at fifteen he was playing on the factory team. But a national habit is pervasive; his mother, for example, a simple woman who worked at the same factory, knew only one way to nurse a man: liquor. Once, when the young athlete broke his leg and landed in the hospital, she smuggled the medicine in on her visits.

Streltsov became a professional player at seventeen. His workday now consisted of warm-up exercises, sprints, weight lifting, theory study (the Soviet Union has scholars and soccer departments at twenty-three institutes of physical education), field technique, and seven miles of cross-country running over rugged terrain or mud or snow. He went at his training program fanatically, and the traditional bottle of brandy became his only means of dealing with the tension. So inexhaustible were his young body's resources that he could drink all night and the next day sprint the whole 90 minutes of a game, defying every law of human chemistry.

By the time he was eighteen, the best of Moscow society was vying to have Streltsov at its parties. Writers, directors, and diplomats would come over just to shake the hero's hand.

It has always been considered an act of the highest valor at Russian parties to down a glass of straight vodka in a single gulp while the spirited crowd chants "Down the hatch!" Streltsov became a champion in this as well, disposing of several shots in a row and establishing his lineage with Russian heroes of legend and lore. And through it all, his level of play remained formidable. Fullbacks would tackle him by the legs, elbow him in the gut, snatch him by the shorts, charge him from behind, pounce on his back, and grab him by the hands, but he suffered it all without a fight and managed always to rout the roughnecks without stooping to their game.

Yet it was thanks to the liquid that at twenty-one—at the peak of his career—Streltsov was given eight years in the slammer.

He accepted the sentence as his due, making no effort to defend himself, telling the judge that whether or not he had been provoked, he had acted like an ungovernable animal and should be punished as such, cleansed of his sins through hard labor.

The Soviet National Team lost the 1958 World Cup and hasn't made even third place since—despite the fact that millions of teenagers are practicing on school fields, thousands of amateurs are running back and forth in factory stadiums, and hundreds of pros are competing in official clubs.

At the beginning of every fiscal year the Sports Committee sends lengthy Finance-Ministry-approved documents to all Soviet soccer clubs with "Top Secret" stamped in the upper right. The documents detail the sums to be paid forwards, midfielders, backs, and goalies—none of whom are supposed to be salaried at all in a country that pretends to universal amateurism.

Depending on their league, players are given from $150 to $300 a month, salaries that can skyrocket upon the order of local party commissars, for whom soccer is an effective administrative tool. Unpublished reports by Soviet socio-economists indicate that increases in industrial output—jumps as great as 50 percent—result not from infusions of ideology but from the victories of local teams.

To escalate the flow of tractors, planes, fertilizers, or drill presses from his region, a commissar—even if he secretly hates the game—must cultivate a passion for soccer, convert his party lieutenants into avid fans, research the possibilities of bribing the referees or the players of the opposing team, and issue memorandums to factory directors on securing more funds per player. If the commissar is inventive enough, a provincial team can surface even in the country's remotest regions. So it was with the Ukrainian city of Voroshilovgrad, whose team won the Soviet championship, or Kaliningrad—not always on the map, but the winner of the Crystal Cup. The players of these teams can make well over $1,000 a month, incomparably more than in any club in the capital city—where, under the shadow of the Kremlin, the bosses have more trouble getting away with their fiscal chicanery.

In any hick town of a hundred thousand there's a stadium built for at least half that number. It makes little difference that the stadium will never draw more than ten thousand spectators and that the soccer club can't possibly pay off financially; all expenses are covered by a clause in the trade-union budget providing an allotment for athletics. Neither is it considered a problem that the players of the club moonlight as fighters whose object it is to K.O. opposing forwards; they're supported by the party line to win at any price. Those who break the most bones can look forward to being handed an envelope by the commissar the next day in the locker room. Nor is it questioned that the Izhevsk city team plays in the same league as Vladivostok's, five thousand miles and several time zones away; the commissar just gets hold of a TU-104. If the team gives a particularly good showing, its players may find themselves in the same jet on the way to Marseilles or Hamburg, for the greater glory of the city—and its commissar—overseas.

If a poor performance leads to a threat of ousting the club from its league, the commissar himself flies off to Moscow to prove to the Sports Committee the crucial importance of his city—the home of, say, missile silos or uranium mines. Via administrative order, the club is retained in the league.

None of this is questioned. But it is thanks to this that soccer has turned into a clumsy, unruly system, matching that of any other bureaucracy in the Communist morass.

Major league soccer in the USSR consists of thirty-six clubs—the top sixteen and the next twenty. Each club is made up of a first-string team, a second-string team, and service personnel—forty members in all—and operates on an annual budget of $2 million. The minor league contains six divisions, comprising ninety-six clubs with budgets, personnel, and stadiums all but indistinguishable from the majors and carving the Soviet Union into islands of ardent enthusiasts. Professional clubs play a total of twenty-two thousand games a year, the continual interchange leading to a general leveling of quality—an abasement of the stronger clubs as much as an elevation of the weaker. Talented players don't care about keeping in shape, knowing that if they're kicked out of the Moscow clubs, they'll be picked up instantly by the provincial ones —possibly with greater privileges. As a result, tough, competitive struggle—the essence of any sport—has vanished from Soviet soccer.

Nikita Khrushchev suffered from an organizational itch, which he scratched by breaking up the ministries and creating national economic councils, dividing general party committees into industrial and agricultural committees, and mercilessly reducing overextended staffs. Time passed, but economic indexes failed to reveal any improvement;

in fact, the number of officials, in a new wrapping, multiplied. In response, Khrushchev constructed a fresh bureaucratic structure, never perceiving that it was the foundation, and not the structure, that needed the revamping.

Like the party chairman, the leaders of the Sports Committee set about an all-out reorganization of sports. They merged, recombined, and dissolved the major and minor leagues, added new stages on the road to the national championship, or halted competitions altogether in Olympic years.

The last twenty years have seen sixteen trainers of the National Team come and go; in the same period, West Germany and England have had just two apiece. This rapid turnover of trainers has sent outstanding specialists packing to the provinces, where they can live peacefully and without the constant scrutiny of Moscow.

When the Soviet Union loses the World Cup, the players of the National Team are rushed back to Moscow like naughty schoolboys, forbidden to stay to watch the finals even at their own expense.

Thanks to an inferiority complex, the bosses of Russian soccer patterned play first after the Brazilians, then after the English, then after the Brazilians again, and lately after the top three teams at Munich—West Germany, Holland, and Poland.

The collective style of play that was once dominant and that made soccer the quintessential Communist sport was converted by ukase to an every-man-for-himself approach. The Russians sowed fear at international matches not for outplaying others technically but for assaulting them physically.

The command descended next to master speed. Soviet

players became the fastest in the world, and still they failed to score.

"Aha!" said some clever functionary. "It's all a question of age." In a matter of a week, the birth certificates of every player in the country were investigated and everyone over thirty was discharged.

Finally, the officials concluded that the decline of soccer in the USSR had most to do with inadequate political indoctrination. A Young Communist organizer was assigned to every club to brainwash the backs and instill the strikers with Marx's theory of the undying struggle between labor and capital.

"Soviet soccer," summarized *Komsomolskaia Pravda*, "above all else requires genuinely good citizens." Accordingly, some of the National Team's best players—Iosif Sabo, Fëdor Medved, Gennadii Krasnitskii, and Viktor Ponedelnik—were expelled on charges such as: "Accepted two apartments and two automobiles"; "Violated the moral code of the builders of Communism"; and "Divorced himself from the working masses." In the wake of propaganda and purges, the National Team, fortified with politically literate and morally stable players, became virtually impotent on the field.

It seemed that every criminal who found himself in a labor camp after 1958 sent a letter home at one time or another reporting that he was a cellmate of Eduard Streltsov, that they had become buddies, and that he was getting lessons in kicking penalty shots.

In the meantime, however, the real Streltsov was doing time in the new industrial city of Elektrostal; after a six-month stay in a Moscow prison, he had been transferred to a chemical combine construction crew.

The Gulag system underwent a radical change toward the end of the 1950s. Prisoners who had demonstrated good behavior behind barbed wire were granted assignments to "chemistry"—the construction of new works for the rapidly developing chemical industry. (The term today has been broadened to include the metallurgical, automobile, and other industries.) Chemistry convicts went unguarded and were allowed to rent rooms or live in workers' dormitories; leaving the city, of course, was prohibited. Although the work was hard and demanding, the laborers received standard remuneration. Streltsov married a waitress from an Elektrostal eatery, and the couple soon had a son.

After six years, Streltsov was released and returned to Moscow. Two world championships had come and gone, soccer strategy and technique had developed, and stunts that once seemed unachievable had become old-fashioned. The national hero's fierce tribe of fans had long since laid his career to rest.

In the spring of 1965 rumors began circulating that Streltsov was going to play for his old club, the Torpedoes, in a game against the Dynamos. A mob of a hundred thousand jammed Luzhniki to pay their respects to the ill-fated athlete—the agony of their former idol eliciting no less excitement than his triumphs once had. The standing ovation that followed his first goal turned the crowd into one family again, thrilled with the return of a stolen national treasure. As they had six years earlier, people began talking not of going to Luzhniki but of going to see Streltsov, just as they spoke not of going to the Bolshoi but to see Plisetskaia.

Even *Komsomolskaia Pravda* acknowledged the phenomenon. Two years in a row—1967 and 1968—they named Streltsov forward of the year. But controversy bubbled just under the surface: though again on the National Team, Streltsov was prohibited from accompanying the team to the European and world championships.

The great player showed his first signs of fatigue in 1970. Streltsov tore the cartilage in both knees, signs developed of chronic inflammation of the joints, and his muscles could no longer support his now heavier body. Like an old soldier, his body ached from the countless blows sustained in years of play. The "Streltsov legend" was so powerful, however, that even inveterate bullies on the field turned into gentlemen and tried to deal with him by the rules. The fans, usually merciless critics, observed an unnatural quiet whenever he slipped up.

Streltsov retired from soccer in 1972 at the age of thirty-five, a living symbol of Russian national character—self-possessed and self-destructive, strong-willed and servile, sentimental and cruel, stoic, heroic, and drunk.

FIVE

The Myth of Mass Sports and the Road to Championship

From the beginning, Lenin envisaged a sports program as imperative in his master plan for the new Soviet nation; if young people were to join the battle for Communism, he declared, it behooved them "to meet the confrontation head on—strong and healthy, with muscles of iron and nerves of steel." Lenin's ideas have come to full flower through the years: sports have been turned into a tank of the true faith, leveled at trammeling the athletic cadres of capitalism.

Soviets have won 658 medals since their 1952 Olympic debut at Helsinki—more than any other nation in the world. Officials ascribe this success to the mass proportions of the enterprise, and the media flaunt impressive figures: fifty million adults are busy with athletics and twenty million children engage in sports at school. In truth, the figures are procured by juggling the statistics.

Like any other Soviet institution, the sports mechanism —from local trainers in Tadzhik truckstops to general managers in Moscow—runs smoothly only so long as an endless stream of reports makes its way uninterrupted to the top. Monthly or quarterly, on competition or training procedures, these reports are all expected to demonstrate two essential and mutually exclusive elements: large numbers of athletes (pure bulk serving as fuel for the propaganda foundry) and top-flight performance (the crucible for Olympic medals).

A coach is entitled to a salary only if he trains at least thirty or forty students. But earning only the usual $150 a month means having to worry about making ends meet; if he cultivates a few top athletes, a coach's economic circumstances soar through prizes, salaried sojourns at training camps, and trips abroad. On the other hand, working with large groups and paying equal attention to everyone cuts into the time available for nurturing the promising few. His life is consumed in shuttling between the Scylla of not training enough people, which is bad, and the Charybdis of not producing champions, which is worse.

Viktor Lonskii, an Honored Coach of the Soviet Union, has commented, "The stampede for mass statistics keeps us from the work we need to do with individuals if we're to turn out A-1 athletes."

Leonid Poliakovskii, a less well known but more pragmatic gymnastics coach who now lives in Los Angeles, recalled, "At the beginning of every year I'd go around to various high schools and collect about forty teenagers to form a group for the Kharkov sports school. By the second or third training session about twenty had dropped out, for various reasons. If I culled one or two talented kids from the ones that remained, I'd work with them alone and let the others know they'd be better off playing soccer on the street. But I'd keep all forty in my reports and even my own log just the same, so my salary was sustained by 'dead souls.' And if the one or two did well, the principal never asked what happened to the others."

Obsessed with numbers, the town fathers of Norilsk, somewhere above the Arctic, would consider themselves ideologically deficient if they supplied the national Spartacus Games with a contingent that was arithmetically inferior to Moscow's. Meanwhile, in Moscow, the managers of a brickworks would be willing to stand on their heads to come up with teams for as many of the twenty Olympic sports as the giant auto plant down the road.

Mass-sports schizophrenia does have its economic benefits for coaches, some of whom hold down six or seven posts at once and fret less over training than about how to scurry from one gym to the next to pick up their paychecks. These moonlighters drag the same handful of good athletes to all of their assignments, so that at a regional meet, student pole-vaulter Ivanov, contending for the agricultural institute, can be slated to confront pole-vaulter Petrov, a pipefitter from a local chemical plant, when both are in fact a single fellow by the name of Sidorov.

A coach from Kiev told me that before every anniversary of the Revolution he'd be ordered to deliver a whole column of Masters of Sport to the parade when he actually had only two for the task. He'd come to the university, hand out dozens of his Spartak uniforms, sit the students on a bus, march them past the government reviewing stand, pay them five dollars apiece, and let them go. A swimming coach from Moscow recounted that he used to bring his girls' team to evening meets at outdoor pools. The light was too dim to show that half his team was made up of young boys.

In September 1976 the Uzbekistan rifle competitions for the *Komsomolskaia Pravda* Prize attracted hundreds of participants who, the paper reported smugly, hit the targets with astounding accuracy. Three months later *Komsomol-skaia Pravda* sanctimoniously blustered over an "outrageous fraud": the bullet holes had been counterfeited in a shooting gallery a week before.

Rural coaches mailed reports to Moscow indicating that a million and a half peasants were members of the Collective Farmer Club. Since the club claimed only five hundred qualified coaches nationwide, to cover that many players every coach would have had to be a wizard on a magic carpet—teaching three thousand farmers in one swoop to cast javelins across corn fields or spike volleyballs amid cow manure.

Olympic champion Pëtr Bolotnikov reported the following: "I once got an honorary invitation to the Russian rural championships in Krasnodar. I couldn't believe my eyes when I looked over the entry forms: there wasn't a tractor driver, combine operator, or milkmaid among them. Not a single real farmer. Every team was made up of gym teachers, coaches, trainers, students, state insurance accountants, products managers, and artists. I didn't know whether I was watching a competition of collective farmers or a convention of imposters."

The greatest folderol is reserved for the widely publicized "Ready for Labor and Defense" (GTO) program, through which every sector of Soviet society is summoned perfunctorily to keep the population fit through participation in some fifty sports. GTO organizes huge spectacles in which energetic phys. ed. instructors throng stadiums with thousands of workers supposed to be vying with each other in running with raised rifles, flinging grenades, climbing up ropes, stumbling across water-filled ditches, clambering over obstacle courses, or swimming fully dressed. Since most workers view these exercises with a somewhat jaundiced eye, they're granted the option of inviting gung-ho nephews or acrobatic uncles to join in the festivities.

Most of the relatives wouldn't dream of coming to the overcrowded stadiums without liquor. Others pack along jars of pickles or buckets of draft beer. The place turns into a huge picnic. By the time the workers are ordered to line up, they stand with their rifles butt first and have trouble telling the start from the finish. Most prefer not to run anyway, instead crawling on all fours while droning the first few bars of "Moscow Nights." That's well and good, as long as they all sign testimonies to having taken part in GTO day.

These testimonies are gathered into overstuffed binders, stamped with the signatures of the local party organizers, and mailed off to the provincial party committees. The higher-ups leaf through pages crowded with the signatures of thousands of rifle runners, grenade flingers, and rope climbers without hesitating to perpetuate the pettifogging. In any case, a move to expose the fraud would be tantamount to suicide: any fall-off in participation would be put down to bad management. They have no alternative but to add a few thousand more nonexistent contestants, paste a red wax seal of Lenin's face onto the books, and mail them posthaste to the appropriate commissar in the regional capital.

In the plush offices of the capital the books are bound into still-heavier volumes, the thousands of athletes having been stretched into hundreds of thousands. Condensed and processed versions of these well-embellished bureaucratic tomes come to rest eventually on the mahogany tables of the heads of the Central Committee of the Communist

Party. And finally the millions of mythic athletes reach their highest glory as the General Secretary extols them from the rostrum of the Kremlin's Hall of Congresses.

If the mass approach to sports in the Soviet Union serves to inflate an ideological balloon, the support of promising young athletes is real and aggressive. For one thing, there are boarding schools for the "Olympic Reserve" where children major in sports. The board of education in every city welcomes proven talents into special sports schools. All clubs have a section where well-known coaches or athletes are engaged to tutor the best of the rookies to shoot pucks, kick balls, throw discuses, punch bags, induce court sense in basketball, and sustain teamwork in water polo.

In recent years a "morphological" technique has been worked out to select young athletes according to biological maturity instead of age. The morphological profile also helps zero in on the sport for which a child is best suited. For example, weight lifters-to-be are winnowed by trunk, arm, and leg length. Long limbs are a liability; short shanks and broad shoulders bode better. For gymnastics, smaller children are chosen to minimize the moment of inertia. Swimmers are singled out by arm and leg length, muscle and fat distribution, and other hydrodynamic factors. The morphological profiles of skiers, track-and-field athletes, and hockey players evince femoral flexibility or sheer brawn.

An athlete who excels on the junior level is gradually permitted a share in the financial pie. A sip from the pool of privilege suggests to the young recruit that he's special, privy to the benefits of the sports fraternity, and gives him the impetus to cling tenaciously to his favored status for the rest of his life. From the very first, a coach introduces the best of his flock to restaurants where they can lunch on red meats and fresh vegetables and dine on fish and fruits that make their less talented schoolmates green with envy. Blue Tokyo-made training suits, a scarcity in the shops, are handed out free, and the tyros strut around in them like members of a superior caste.

Victories at city or provincial events draw invitations to spend two or three months at training camps in the country, eating plenty of food and getting the best coaching and medical attention available. A boy who becomes a republic champion in boxing, volleyball, or basketball, or comes in first, second, or third in wrestling or hockey, or does well in track and field, skiing, or speed skating becomes a candidate for Master of Sport—a designation conferred upon one in hundreds and signaling the end of amateurism and the beginning of a life full of the advantages enjoyed by the pros.

The door is now open to the university or institute of his or her choice. Even if the regular admissions ratio is one in ten, twenty, or fifty applicants, the athlete is assured a place, often without having to take the rigorous entrance exams. Once at school, he's handed not only the regular $75 monthly stipend but an extra $80 or $120 off the record from Burevestnik, the university trade-union organization (the average worker makes $160). In a practice that recalls the tradition at big universities in America, even the most demanding professors replace the usual exam questions with ones about the finer points of a recent ballgame or the hardships of marathon running. If an odd pedagogue still dares give one of the stars a low grade, the rector calls him on the carpet and informs him that it's the stars, and not the professors, who are essential to the well-being of the institution. Even if an athlete takes an interest in the treasures of scholarship, he's simply too busy, having to spend six months of the year in training camp and six at tournaments: local, republic, all-Union, and international. An athlete without academic ambitions is set up in a job according to who sponsors his club: electricians, drivers, stonemasons, fishermen, cooks, or carpenters. No one ever sees him on the job, even though every month he's handed $160 in a sealed envelope.

Best off financially are the trade-union clubs, such as Spartak, the Zeniths, and the Miners, who come by their coin along three routes. First, the Council of Ministers of the USSR is authorized to support them by the "development of physical education" clause in the State Budget; second, deductions are required of every industrial, research, or cultural organization amounting to .15 percent of the total salary of its personnel (some clubs, such as Spartak, latch onto 2 or 3 percent of the profits of the factories they represent); and third, dues are paid by the club's members—many of whom never join a gym or take a plunge in a pool but put in a ruble or two as a token of their Socialist commitment to "collective activity."

Statistics boast that trade-union-club expenditures came to $2.5 billion between 1970 and 1975 alone. If the Soviet press usually exaggerates, here the figures were kept low to emphasize that popular enthusiasm, rather than a fountain of funds, keeps socialist sports afloat.

The minute he turns eighteen, every young male athlete, regardless of the club he belongs to, becomes the prey of the Army Sports Club. In point of fact, the entire system's aim is touted as the creation of a strong army. Every athlete is considered a soldier, ready at a moment's notice to line up with ten million other trained troopers to crawl across

Arctic wastes, Saharan sands, or European plains. But when a gifted athlete is drafted into the army, he's not burdened by having to study the techniques of modern warfare or perform defense-oriented exercises; instead, he's given every opportunity to pursue his athletic career as before.

Half a dozen years ago army colonels had to rack their brains to place sports stars as company clerks, regiment musicians, or division quartermasters. But former minister of defense Marshal Andrei Grechko, tired of the pretense, decided to do things out in the open and ordered that every garrison have a sports batallion. Today, when an athlete is drafted, he's immediately given the rank of sergeant and provided $60 a month, uniforms and civvies, separate dorm housing, and freedom to come and go with his comrades at all hours—as long as he brings back a medal or title from time to time.

The whole defense budget being a state secret, it's hard to know just how many millions the army earmarks for sports. Since its club regularly routs all others at every sport, since its athletes accounted for some 40 percent of the Soviet national teams at both Munich and Montreal, and since it has the best facilities and most expensive equipment, a modest estimate of its budget would run in the range of at least a quarter of a billion dollars a year.

The country's second most prestigious club is the Dynamos, who represent the state security organizations— the KGB and the police. The Dynamos are the only club the government doesn't subsidize: their funds derive from the income of prison factories, work camps, forced-labor industries, and confiscated private estates (the KGB officially puts this at an unlikely $30 million; the real figure probably exceeds several times that).

One reason athletes are especially eager to join a **Dynamo** team is that state security entails the customs service: virtually all team members are exempt from border customs control. Boxer Grigorii Rogalskii, a former Leningrad champion and Master of Sport now living in New York, told me this story:

"I once had occasion to go to West Germany. Like every athlete traveling abroad, I had to get my documents in order. I was twenty-six and a member of neither Komsomol nor the party, and you had to belong to one or the other to go overseas. But I had a damn good right hook, and they didn't have time to replace me. I was admitted to Komsomol in the matter of a day. They even reconciled themselves to my being Jewish. They took our team, the Leningrad Dynamos, to the Foreign Travel Section of the Central Committee, on Granovskii Street in Moscow. First we signed a promise not to reveal the content of the talk we were about to have. Then a man came into the office and introduced himself: 'I'm Comrade Ivanov.' We burst out laughing [Ivanov is as common as Smith is in America and often used when someone doesn't want his real name known].

" 'But my name really *is* Ivanov,' he continued, and then spent an hour explaining that we live in a country that's building Communism, and we're going to one that's a showcase of the West. 'You're going to see prosperity and abundance over there,' he said, 'but don't ever forget that we've suffered the terrible destruction of World War II.' (Where are the great mysteries I'm not supposed to divulge? I thought to myself.) 'Ivanov' then gave us a list of people we weren't supposed to associate with: White Russians, Vlasov Army traitors, and, of course, Zionists— all the standard propaganda.

"Although I knew we could take along as much caviar and vodka as we wanted, I really began to appreciate being in the Dynamos after we piled into the bus at the Hotel Central on Gorky Street and headed for Sheremetevo international airport. Instead of waiting in the usual customs lines, a KGB major accompanying the team just waved our papers at the guards and drove us right through to the gates without our ever getting off the bus. When we boarded the Lufthansa jet, our luggage was still untouched by customs. We were home free.

"In Cologne they broke the team into 'troikas'—groups of three—the first day and ordered us to 'see the sights,' which meant one thing: Unload your caviar and vodka. I had twenty bottles of Stolichnaia and four five-pound tins of black beluga. I probably sold them to the very Vlasov traitors Comrade 'Ivanov' warned us against. The same day I bought fifteen pairs of jeans, six Seiko watches, and four auto cassette recorders—the last strictly *verboten*, particularly in wholesale quantities. But everybody did the same, stuffing their suitcases while our KGB major pretended not to see. On our return to Sheremetevo a bus picked us up at the plane and whisked us off to our hotel. The trip netted three thousand rubles—enough to live well on in Russia for a year."

One player, a member of Moscow's soccer Dynamos, became a millionaire by shuttling loads of gold coins in from the West. In the sixties a czarist ten-ruble gold coin brought $22 on the London market. The soccer player would pick up American currency on the sly in Moscow, at about three rubles to the dollar. When he went abroad for a match, he'd buy a hundred coins. Back in Moscow, he'd sell them to Georgian or Central Asian operators, who eagerly paid him 250 rubles apiece. His net profit per coin came to just under 185 rubles, or 18,500 per trip. He averaged ten trips a year.

Not all Dynamos get involved in the black market on such a large scale, but even the most timorous can't resist tossing in a dozen cans of ski wax when packing up their gear for home (a $1.99 can can bring a whopping $30 in Moscow).

A Moscow Dynamos executive I knew whose sole function was to accompany sports delegations overseas began his career as a Master of Sport in fencing. Lacking any outstanding victories, he wisely switched to the cushier position of sports administrator. In ten years he'd become a party member, a KGB colonel, and the owner of an Alfa Romeo. He landed his wife a job as a stewardess on an IL-62 flying between Moscow and New York. He carpeted his apartment with Macy's rugs, outfitted his bathrooms with Crane fixtures, cluttered his wife's closets with dresses from Saks, and strewed his coffee table with copies of *Playboy.* Out of uniform but never reluctant to let it be known he was a KGB colonel (all Dynamos are officers), the executive ran into just one snag: keeping up his Alfa.

Spare parts for foreign cars are a priceless commodity in Russia. Having no taste for the black market, the sports colonel devised new methods of supply. Arriving in Belgium or Italy in his Alfa Romeo (traveling to a foreign country in one's private car is the rarest of honors and provided only to the most trusted operators in the KGB), he'd make a deal with the local entrepreneur: they'd install a new transmission, tires, or carburetor in his car, and he'd promise on his next visit to deliver antique enamel or silver ladles picked up from peasants in the Arkhangelsk area for a hunk of salami.

One more advantage of belonging to the Dynamos is

that its members have permits to live in Moscow, Leningrad, and Kiev: the internal passport system, established by none other than the KGB, denies other newcomers to these towns the status of permanent residence. Even if a person has a place to live, he can't stay there without a stamp in his passport called a *propiska*. The very restriction intrigues the provincial population like forbidden fruit, but much more alluring is the big cities' incomparably better standard of living. Unlike many small towns in America, where one can be sure of getting the same Texaco gasoline, McDonald's cheeseburgers, and Hanes pantyhose as in New York, a small Russian city is a wasteland when it comes to buying anything from bread to sports equipment. Just the chance to live in Moscow is considered the most desirable promotion possible. Only a handful make it. And, to do so, athletes must be willing to leave the Perm Spartaks or the Odessa Burevestniks for the Moscow Dynamos.

There are no contracts, no free agents, and no powerful lawyers in Soviet sports. Clubs have no regulations regarding trades—except in soccer, where the most sought-after players negotiate their own terms every December. But the athletic market is like a year-end sale: a lot of noise, but not much merchandise to be had. The big stars are held virtually under house arrest during the period, while promising rookies are rerouted to the army for a month's "special training."

Hustler clubs in other sports rely on scouts to restock their stores. With pockets full of cash, the scout comes around and tries by hook or by crook to separate the best athletes from their teams. The scout may live in Dnepropetrovsk or Leningrad, but when he turns up at a track meet or basketball game in Rostov or Minsk the coaches spot him right off and panic like swimmers at the sight of a shark.

There isn't much to be done when a scout shows his face. As a rule, he's already marked his prey and wields a dossier in his satchel detailing sensitive information about the star's early indiscretions and any problems in deportment with his parents, girls, or coach. The scout may already have chatted with him somewhere out of earshot in a park, and the great erstwhile hope of the locals may already have agreed to desert—with the promise of a Fiat-124, paint still fresh, awaiting his arrival.

The athlete's anxious guardians will sometimes appeal to the director. If he can't outbid the stranger, he'll have the scout thrown out of his hotel and beaten to a pulp in a dark alley. In retaliation, three muscle-bound bruisers from the big team will kidnap the prize and make him send back a telegram a few days later rhapsodizing about his new home. Athletic abductions have become a disease of Soviet sports: coaches have lost interest in grooming their best athletes, who they know are going to be stolen anyway, half-way through training, by the more flamboyant clubs. The press has published countless critiques enjoining the sports world to abide by Communist moral principles and to safe-guard athletics from the tyranny of these sports "patrons" —without ever actually exposing the real culprits. But everyone, from fan to rookie to veteran, knows that the patrons are none other than the provincial party secre-taries, who turn athletes into paid gladiators and heed newspaper complaints no more than they would the whistle of a distant train.

One of the most successful of these sports scavengers was Vladimir Shevchenko, the secretary of the Voroshilov-grad Party Committee. With a few rubles, Shevchenko reeled in the brilliant Moscow soccer coach Konstantin Beskov and the outstanding Kiev forward Iosif Sabo, eventually to garner a spectacular winning streak for the Voroshilovgrad Sunrises.

World champion gymnast Viktor Lisitskii and world-class weight lifter Stanislav Batishchev, Olympic rowing champions and European volleyball medalists, all succumbed to the pecuniary pressure of Shevchenko's scouts to grace the streets of Voroshilovgrad with permanent residence.

The demise of the secretary's career came unexpectedly. Central Committee inspectors sent by Vladimir Shcherbitskii, one of Shevchenko's enemies in the Politburo, turned up evidence that the secretary had been robbing the Kremlin blind by misappropriating funds from the party coffers not only for paying fantastic fees but for enhancing his personal fortune as well. In a rare, publicized scandal, on December 15, 1973, Shevchenko was resoundingly given the boot.

In the wake of the Shevchenko affair it was decided to introduce a double accounting system that would split points and credits between different coaches. A trainer who had backed a boxer for Spartak would get a share of the points his pupil later compiled with the Army Club, and eight university Burevestnik rowers would distribute a percentage of their points among the eight clubs they had belonged to before coming to campus. This sharing of accomplishments has enabled both old and new coaches to continue sending impressive reports to the top and enjoying its financial rewards.

Year-round competitive fever has kept coaches busy and created a national network of ringers—often Masters of Sport (a title conferred in official competition on a sprinter who runs 100 meters in 10.4 seconds or 200 meters in 21.4, a high jumper who clears 6′ 6¾″, or a long-jumper who makes 25 feet). From either lack of ambition or unwillingness to work, these ringers fail to yield consistently top results. But club managers, confident they'll produce just enough to earn the club its life-supporting points, hire them to have on hand for the big events. The ringers themselves switch clubs a dozen times and earn about 3,500 under-the-table rubles a year. Considering that the Soviet Union has about forty-five thousand active Masters of Sport and that only about a thousand are tied up in training for the Olympics, ringers are quite an industry.

The Physical Culture and Sports Committee of the Council of Ministers of the USSR (or, more simply, the Sports Committee), though nominally the highest governmental body responsible for the physical fitness of the Soviet Union's 270 million people, is actually occupied solely with the selection, training, and long-range development of Olympic teams. The committee's budget of $35 million comes from twelve sports equipment factories, the nation's leading sports newspaper (*Sovetskii Sport*; circulation, four million), and the highly successful sports lottery.

The Sports Committee spends a large part of its income on maintaining its bureaucratic apparatus—particularly on the highly paid state coaches and their staffs, many of whom were once famous athletes themselves—Arkadii Vorobëv and Aleksei Medvedev in weight lifting, Igor Ter-Ovanesian in track and field, Arkadii Chernyshëv in hockey, Larisa Latynina in gymnastics, and Aleksandr Vedenin in figure skating, to name a few. As athletic watchdogs, they keep a constant eye on the entire competitive scene, so that even in a remote Middle Asian city, separated from civilization by the sands of the Kara-Kum, no really promising athlete goes unnoticed.

Of course, to locate an athlete is one thing; it's quite another to tear him away from the local taskmasters and remove him to Moscow's elite training establishment. It's not at all surprising that the party bosses of Khabarovsk or Kishinëv are reluctant to turn their prize weight lifter into an Olympic champion: they take it for granted that once he tastes the *dolce* Moscow *vita* he'll never come back.

State coaches can't resort to kidnappings, nor do they have the clout to get through to party secretaries. Centuries ago Russia was divided into principalities by militant feudal lords, and it's not much different with today's party executives and their provinces. In the early 1960s Nikita Khrushchev, following in the footsteps of Ivan the Terrible and Peter the Great, tried to crush the power of the local princes. Khrushchev resettled the party chiefs from private estates into public compounds and designed a system restricting a secretary's tenure to four years. It happens that the majority of the party's Central Committee consists of provincial secretaries, who banded together and toppled the Boss in October 1964.

All the state coaches can do is complain to the Sports Committee chairman. Since 1968 this has been an influential member of the Central Committee of the Communist Party: Sergei Pavlov, forty-seven, a short, ruddy, well-fed, youthful-looking man with a benevolent smile. In 1954, while a boxing student at Moscow's Institute of Physical Culture, Pavlov struck Khrushchev as an activist and was elevated to the position of Moscow Komsomol secretary, where he used his powerful uppercuts and sharp, quick jabs to K.O. young dissidents. The poet Yevgenii Yevtushenko has written that the

> Apple-cheeked Komsomol leader
> Taught me to write verses
> Jabbing his fist into my soul . . .

Pavlov's pugilistic prowess was recognized properly in 1959, when he was appointed general secretary of Komsomol. But it wasn't long before he was corrupted by the very bourgeois influences he was supposed to be fighting. In 1968 it was revealed that Komsomol's financial commodore had been covering up expenses incurred by Pavlov's insatiable sexual appetite. Pavlov was about to join his early benefactor Khrushchev as a nonperson when he was taken under the wing of Leonid Brezhnev and rose from the canvas to become Soviet sports czar. Winner and still champion, now fashionably dressed and a bit more tolerant, he's affected a liberal air in an effort to curry international regard. Recently he hired the intelligent, refined, English-speaking Vitalii Smirnov as his deputy, dispatching him to represent the Soviets on the International Olympic Committee to make sure the Communists would hold their own amid the committee's dukes and barons.

In the course of selecting Olympic teams, Pavlov finds himself knocking not dissidents' heads but those of his party comrades. Now a member of the Central Committee, he castigates recalcitrant secretaries for "antipatriotic behavior" or "sacrificing the country's interests for the sake of despicable private purposes." His last resort, when a situation gets really deadlocked, is a direct appeal to Brezhnev.

When not feuding with the Communist princes, Pavlov deals with the board of directors of the Sports Committee in his efforts to facilitate the progress of promising athletes on the road to the Olympics. The committee members include the deputy chairman of trade unions, the deputy

minister of defense, the deputy chairman of the KGB, the
secretary of Komsomol, the deputy minister of education,
the deputy minister of culture, representatives of the largest
industrial ministries, and even the vice-president of the
Academy of Sciences. Conditioned by Pavlov (no relation
to the late physiologist), this group has learned to fish
athletes out of the nation's remotest backwater ponds.

The Sports Committee administers all the trade-union
clubs, the Army Sports Club, and the Dynamos—not so
much in their everyday dealings as in the strategic disburse-
ment and balancing of their billion-dollar budget. In
Kazakhstan, $25 million was sunk into the construction of
a mountain skating complex called Medeo, and sports clubs
in Armenia forked over $30 million toward the establish-
ment of a winter and summer Olympic camp called
Tsakhkadzor. All together, the nation's clubs have con-
tributed untold millions to erect a chain of Olympic
training complexes along some 25 miles of Black Sea shore-
line between the resort towns of Adler and Sochi.

Authorities send their athletes for acclimatization to
areas of the country where the weather approximates that
of an upcoming Olympic site. In 1956 they evicted people
from hotels in Tashkent to make room for athletes training
for Melbourne; in 1964 they uprooted part of the population of the Far Eastern port of Nakhodka to install athletes
bound for Tokyo; in 1968 they built the high-altitude
south Armenian Tsakhkadzor to match the climate of
Mexico City.

In February 1972 my filmmaking activities took me to
Tsakhkadzor, which by then had been turned into a winter
and summer Olympic base. Though the camp had been
operating for four years, it seemed like nothing so much
as New York during a power failure. Despite below-zero

temperatures the rooms were unheated, and the manager kept explaining that the place had never been designed for pampered movie types but for athletes, who needed to steel themselves to the cold and spend their nights in sleeping bags. Immense ski runs and jumps were available in early morning, but by afternoon the lifts broke down under the stepped-up traffic. I didn't meet a single National Team skier using Soviet equipment, except maybe to whack the restaurant manager over the head when the food was bad. Inside the gyms the body-building apparatus would have been below par for any American health spa. All in all, Tsakhkadzor was a typical Soviet enterprise: millions invested enthusiastically at the outset, followed by failure to work out the details.

Pavlov, who was well aware of the vulnerability of any project entailing sophisticated equipment and constant maintenance, wrote off in advance any possibility of Olympic victories in downhill racing, slalom, bobsledding, or jumping, and aimed instead at gold in cross-country skiing and speed skating: Russians have plenty of snow and lots of natural rinks.

Olympic planning in Russia focuses not on a sport's popularity but on other countries' weakness in it. Several years ago handball was unheard of, and canoeing and kayaking were known mainly through tales of American Indians and Eskimos. But canny committee strategists gave the word to Pavlov that they could lead to easy gold. A directive was dispatched to twenty-three physical culture institutes, twenty-five sports colleges, and eighty-five university phys. ed. departments to offer crash courses for *gandbolisty, kanoisty,* and *kayakisty* and then to cultivate the sports by competing against each other during the next five-year plan. The result: six gold medals in kayaking and canoeing at Munich, and six more, plus both gold medals in handball, at Montreal.

The Sports Committee pays a thousand Olympics-bound men and women $5 million annually to spare them the headache of working for a living. For eleven months of the year they train in the nation's best stadiums and gyms, ride the trains of the Locomotives sports club, sail the ships of the Water Transport Workers' Union Club, fly the planes of the Army Club, wear imported clothes delivered from Spartak's warehouses, eat the produce of the Collective Farmer Club, and live in the hotels of the Dynamos—all free of charge. Then, for one month a year, they're given GPT (General Physical Training) in Sochi or Tsakhkadzor, which amounts to a paid vacation, complete with sunbathing, dancing, drinking, and sex, to inspire them for another year of hard work. When they get back from the Olympics, medals clanking in their pockets, the champions are candidates for cars through the Torpedoes, the auto-union club, and apartments through the Construction Workers. They may even be decorated with an Order of Lenin by Chairman Pavlov himself.

The Sports Committee's Scientific and Methodological Council operates laboratories in its physical culture institutes that conduct research in all sciences touching on sports. The object is to exploit human potential to its fullest.

While the current practice of milking everything out of an athlete during his peak and then forgetting him is the same as it was with world champion Vladimir Kuts twenty years ago, at least the physical research methods are more elaborate, and in some ways the apparatus is more advanced than in the West. The case of Olympic champion Valerii

Borzov (gold medals in the 100 and 200 meters at Munich and a bronze for the 100 at Montreal) and his trainer, Valentin Petrovskii (a Ph.D. in biology), shines through the haze of official exaggeration as an interesting example.

In predicting the chances of capturing gold medals, Sports Committee strategists had given up on Borzov, since his trainer's methods flew in the face of all their hallowed standards. Petrovskii had categorically rejected the practice of training athletes "to storm world records" (even forbidding the expression) and stepping up training before major meets. Instead of "You must" he used "Let's try." He made running a joy for the runner, not a point of pride for the motherland.

To Petrovskii, a sprinter was a machine that operated on two interconnecting channels: biomechanical and biochemical. He began working with Borzov by measuring the angle of flexion of his legs and the inclination of his body at every phase of a race. He checked the runner's movements against filmstrips of world-class sprinters, made corrections, and computed Borzov's optimal biomoments. For convenient daily comparison of Borzov's data with the world's best, Petrovskii drew up a table listing examples of his times for certain distances:

	30 m (running)	30 m (from starting block)	60 m (from starting block)	100 m (from starting block)
Time in	2.5	3.5	6.5	10.1
seconds	2.6	3.6	6.6	10.3
	2.7	3.7	6.7	10.5
	2.8	3.8	6.8	10.7

If the sprinter failed to clock the time the coach required for the midsection 30 meters, Petrovskii concluded that his pupil just lacked speed. Failure to make it for the starting 30, even though the other three figures were adequate, suggested something was wrong with his starting technique. If the runner didn't satisfy his standard for the 60 or 100, endurance was the problem. When his protégé began showing steady results for the first three categories, Petrovskii would bring all the statistics together for amazingly accurate predictions of the time for the entire race.

During the 1970 season Petrovskii's table indicated that although Borzov's endurance had improved noticeably, his speed had begun to decline. Puzzled, the coach taped sensors to the sprinter's body to pick up data on his oxygen metabolism, muscular activity, and nervous function during running and at rest. Comparison of the two led him to conclude that heavy daily workouts were contraindicated.

Most world-class sprinters put in five hours of legwork a day in either three mornings and six evenings or four mornings and five evenings a week. Petrovskii prescribed only four sessions a week, never in more than one two-hour stint per twenty-four hours.

Although the state coaches and their watchdogs had crossed Borzov off their list of Olympic prospects, the pair paid no attention. In fact, if Petrovskii noticed Borzov's time improving on its own, ahead of schedule, he insisted that the sprinter take it slower.

Again using his table, Petrovskii tested Borzov on the Tartan track at Munich and found his performance significantly slower than on cinder. Adjusting to the Tartan required fundamental changes in technique. It took eight months.

The sports functionaries were beginning to forget about the obstinate pair, but Petrovskii was polishing off the finishing touches. He trained Borzov to fight a starting headwind by pressing his own hands against the sprinter's shoulders while still in the starting position and keeping them there for the first few strides after the gun.

To limber him up before a training heat, Petrovskii had the sprinter face backwards, spring into a handstand and lightly bound off the ground from his palms, straighten up to full height, leap into a twist and, barely alighting on the track, dash off the remaining meters to the tape. For actual events, the trainer designed what looked like a delayed start. Borzov would run bent low to the track for the first few strides, giving his 170-pound body a thrust like that of a rocket after takeoff. Laying slightly behind the other sprinters, who had straightened up at the gun and moved into full tilt, Borzov picked up his pace only after six strides—exploding forward and easily outrunning his opponents. He mastered a smooth, distinctive finish kick, never having to lean into the tape.

The Sports Committee observers were amazed when Borzov took the European winter championships in 1972. They were stunned by his success at the USSR championships. And by his triumph at Munich they were ready to put his coach, Petrovskii, in the pantheon of pure genius.

Steroids are neither provided nor officially sanctioned by the Sports Committee, but the pills—testosterone derivatives that can be synthesized in the laboratory—are used by some coaches for certain athletes. In clinical medicine, anabolic steroids have been used successfully to treat dystrophies, serious injuries, and disturbances of protein metabolism. In the mid-sixties they flooded the world sports market as an easy means of intensifying protein synthesis in the muscles and thereby accelerating metabolism and activity. By the seventies, sports medicine had begun to record a growing list of negative effects, but it was already too late to halt steroid consumption or to check with accuracy on who was taking them and who wasn't.

I talked with Arvids Iserlis, a former rowing coach and associate of the Soviet national crew for the Olympics who emigrated to New York in 1975: "Six years ago I got hold of some Hungarian-made anabolites and began giving two pills a day to the women in the quadruple sculls. After three months the girls' arms and legs were quite obviously larger. The pills were working.

"I provided them only for short periods, when the athletes wanted them, and after consulting with doctors. Some physicians feel that periodic use has no significant systemic effect; others claim that regular, prolonged consumption carries the risk of impotence in men, infertility in women, and an insidious decline in general health. The example of Vasilii Alekseev, the weight lifter, contradicts this."

"You mean he definitely took steroids, and they helped him, with no bad effects?" I asked.

"Well, it's only a guess, of course, since I never saw him down any with my own eyes. But within the inner circle of Soviet trainers we exchanged a lot of information, and the word was that he got his weight up from two twenty to three forty-four—and that's a hundred and twenty-four pounds of muscle, not fat—by using steroids. And after six years of setting records he still seemed inexhaustible."

"All right, but assuming he did take steroids, how did he get through the steroid tests at the Montreal Olympics? According to the papers, they gave him a particularly close examination."

"Well, you have to realize, an athlete reaches his peak

muscle tone a month or two before competition. After-wards, he doesn't have to keep building himself up, so he can cut out the pills. The thing about steroids is that the testing has to be done fairly soon after they've been used. But since the steroids were last taken a month or more before, they've long since been decomposed by the liver and eliminated with the urine—without a trace. There's nothing left to detect.

"I think a lot of Soviet athletes are on anabolites now, and their Western counterparts, too. The reason is simple: new records are being set every year, and they're getting harder and harder to break. Drugs can't create good per-formances in themselves, but when everything else is equal—desire, physical strength, skill, stamina—they can make the difference. If steroids are going to be properly detected at the Moscow Olympics, I think the IOC testing equipment will have to be reoriented toward finding not the steroid itself but the more lasting effects it has on the body. They could check the hormonal balance, which is very sensitive and shows signs of chemical involvement even if it isn't altered substantially itself. Otherwise, sports will become a competition between the best pills, not the best people."

"But again, the IOC doctors are supposed to be compe-tent professionals. Why did they keep using equipment they knew couldn't detect steroids?" I asked.

"Well, I think they weren't looking so much for steroids —although they did find three cases of recent use and probably missed dozens more—but for hard-core stuff, like real narcotics.

"There's no drug control at Soviet meets. Some athletes, for the sake of making an Olympic team, will swallow or inject anything to give themselves a possible edge. In 1972

I was at one of the big international regattas with the men's quadruple sculls. The morning of the final heat I called the team into the locker room, opened a handsome box with foreign words on the cover, and handed each guy a white tablet. I told them that these pills were the last word in ups—undetectable, but more powerful than anything of their kind.

"The team took the heat, no sweat. Later they all said that even by a thousand meters they felt as limber as at the start. Imagine their surprise when I told them the white tablets were nothing but sodium bicarbonate—simple baking powder."

In the 1967 European track-and-field championships, all the women participants were checked for sex. The only one to run afoul was the Polish sprinter Ewa Klobukowska; examination of her chromosomes cast doubt upon her femininity. The case received a great deal of publicity, and in 1968 the IOC rescinded the gold medal she had won at the 1964 Olympics. The Soviet track-and-field authorities quietly withdrew Tamara Press (winner of two gold medals at Tokyo), her sister, Irina (gold medal in the pentathlon at Tokyo), and Maria Itkina (European champion in the 200-meter dash), without even having them tested by the IOC. The names of all three abruptly disappeared from the papers. World-record high jumper Iolanda Balaš of Rumania vanished from the international arena at the peak of her career. In 1952 and 1956, before there was an IOC medical commission, the USSR gained a few Olympic medals through Aleksandra Chudina. She also won several championships in volleyball. Chudina eventually retired without incident.

All these athletes shared certain secondary male characteristics. Irina Press and Itkina had to shave regularly or grow intimidating mustaches and beards. Tamara Press's shoulders, abdomen, arms, and legs were the envy of every male wrestler and weight lifter. Chudina had the long arms and tall, gangly build of a cowboy. She didn't have the slightest hint of breasts, and she spoke with the gruff voice of a man—which she used unabashedly on the volleyball court to order her teammates around.

Their sexual preferences vacillated between male and female. Irina Press dated men and had a husband, from whom she later separated, but her sister Tamara had a charming blond girlfriend whom she brought along to Olympic training camps and lived with in a private room.

The most scandalous story concerned Chudina and her friend, one of the most beautiful girls in Soviet sports— Olympic and three-time world-champion speed skater Inga Artamonova-Voronina. Their friendship took on such dimensions that Inga's husband, Gennadii Voronin, himself a Master of Sport in speed skating, threatened to kill her if she refused to give up Aleksandra. Not believing him, Inga continued to be seen with Chudina. On February 22, 1966, Inga was found on the stairway of her home with her throat slashed. Voronin was given ten years.

A number of women athletes once submitted an indignant letter to the Sports Committee about the injustice of having to compete against men in women's clothing. They were ordered to keep their mouths shut.

Wilma Rudolph, the champion American sprinter, once told me: "I remember the Press sisters very well. In Rome we used to be puzzled by their mannish appearance. Why didn't the Russian doctors treat them with female hormones?"

To go through hormone therapy or sex-change surgery

in order to become full-fledged females would have meant losing their physical prowess and athletic superstardom. On the other hand, it's unthinkable in the Soviet Union to admit publicly to any deviation from the sexual norm, whether inherited or artificially achieved.

The Sports Committee has a propaganda bureau, but this accounts for just a drop in the bucket of the swill Russians have to swallow while watching television, listening to the radio, and reading the papers. There are two basic approaches to this propaganda: either dull descriptions of the events mixed with criticism of negligent factory managers who produce lousy soccer shoes, coaches overburdened with work, and athletes playing around with girls; or, on the other hand, glorification of the values of the New Soviet Man, who in this case happens to be involved in sports. In 1970 a group of Soviet Olympic gold medalists was invited to a round-table discussion sponsored by *Komsomolskaia Pravda*. Two questions were asked: "What helped you win at the Olympics?" and "What is Olympic mettle?" Here are some of the answers:

Valerii Brumel, high jumper: "A rare sense of solidarity, a feeling of togetherness. The whole team was charged with incredible resolve. We all approached the starting line as if we had wings. I'd call it the wings of collectivism."

Alevtina Kolchina, cross-country skier: "A sense of the extraordinary unity of all our country's athletes and the understanding that the people, the motherland, is counting on us to win."

Valerii Popinchenko, boxer: "For me, an Olympic athlete is someone who's capable of putting himself out all the way, aiming all his moral and physical resources at victory."

Aleksandr Ivanitskii, wrestler: "The winner's the guy that's got a broad understanding of life and what he owes to his comrades and country."

Maria Isakova, speed skater: "As I raced along the ice I never forgot for a moment that I was representing Soviet sports and carrying its banner."

One endless tune, prerecorded in all Soviets so that wherever they are, at home in Minsk or abroad in Oslo, they broadcast the same thing, whether or not they believe it and whether or not they're aware of how inauthentic it comes off. And they never go beyond what they're allowed to say, limits they learn from earliest childhood. The journalists pick up their right-minded and familiar words, build them into their stories, and dispatch them through the media for millions, who will laugh at the hypocrisy in the morning and solemnly and shamelessly repeat it all at party meetings in the afternoon.

The highwater mark of Soviet patriotism was proclaimed by the media the day marathoner Hubert Piarnakivi ran at a U.S.-USSR meet in Philadelphia in July 1959. The score stood at 75–73 in favor of the United States, with a 10,000 meters to go that would decide the meet. It was 100 degrees in the shade, with 70 percent humidity. A relentless sun glanced steadily off the metal stands onto the arena, turning the whole stadium into a Turkish bath. Running for the U.S. were Max Truex and Bob Soth; for the USSR, Aleksei Desiatchikov and Piarnakivi. The Soviet pair took the front immediately. Soth took up the challenge, but Truex maintained his slower pace. Halfway through the race Soth was still on the Russian's heels. In the seventh kilometer Desiatchikov, an athlete of exceptional endurance, began a spurt. Piarnakivi paced him and pulled 50 meters ahead of Soth. A

victory for the two Russians—and for the Soviet team—
seemed a certainty when, during the eighth kilometer,
Piarnakivi unexpectedly began to fall back. Heatstroke
had him staggering like a drunk from one side of the track
to the other. The thousands of spectators had risen to
cheer Soth on to pass the hobbling Piarnakivi. The American spurted and overtook the Russian, but not for long.
In the ninth kilometer Soth, too, was seized by heatstroke,
and the stadium began to witness a finish unparalleled in
track history for drama and near tragedy.

Like a butterfly in the wind, Soth lapsed into short,
choppy strides, getting nowhere, and finally fell. Piarnakivi
was lifting his feet convulsively, churning up the track with
his legs, but somehow he kept going. Soth picked himself
up, looking half dead, his eyes glazed and rolling. After a
few steps he toppled over again and lay paralyzed on the
track until he was carried off on a stretcher. Meanwhile
Piarnakivi—half conscious, dehydrated, all the salt sweated
out of his body—continued his tightrope act, swaying,
spiraling jerkily along the track. With 600 meters to go, he
imagined himself only 200 away from the tape. He seemed
to move into a finish kick when he realized there was still
a lap to run. With silent determination he returned to his
suicidal dance.

At a press conference the next day Piarnakivi was asked
what had kept him moving. He answered, "I was always
taught to finish a race at any cost. But most of all, I knew
the victory of the Soviet team depended on my making it."

A friend of mine was a photojournalist for many years
with *Soviet Union* magazine (printed in Helsinki for
foreign distribution, with romantic glossies and glowing
descriptions of the life of Siberian welders—presumably

designed to make workers on the Alaska pipeline agitate for Communist revolution). He now lives in New York and told me the following story:

"Chairman Pavlov once got the idea of showing Western readers how one of his subordinates, Uzbek Sports Committee chairman Amin Aminov, runs athletics in his republic. He called my editor and soon I was on my way. I landed in Tashkent, the capital of Uzbekistan. I had hardly set my feet on the ground when I found myself in the embrace of a jolly man who turned out to be Aminov himself. In the terminal I was hugged by the entire board of directors. A dozen limousines were waiting on the street. Our cavalcade went not to a hotel but straight to a government villa outside the city. I was the only occupant of the thirty-five-room palace. The maid who turned down my bed that night informed me casually, 'You know the prime minister of India, Lal Bahadur Shastri? He slept in this bed.'

" 'That's interesting,' I said.

" 'By the way, he died here, too.'

"The next morning our cortege set off for the town of Chirchik. We arrived at a beautiful garden with tables set for two hundred. The pilaf was steaming, the shashlik was sizzling, and the smell of shishkebab made my mouth water. Toasts were pronounced in my honor. We ate. We drank.

"The next morning we visited a collective farm. Once again the lamb was sliced and the brandy poured . . . Servants passed around hors d'oeuvres. Everything was delicious.

" 'Listen,' I said to Aminov. 'When are we going to start working? Where are your athletes?'

" 'Don't worry,' he answered. 'I've passed the order to

my boys. They're going to take fifty rolls of film. I'm sure you'll find a couple of good shots out of that.'

"After a week of this high living I became sick. I gazed sadly at my bed and thought, I'm going to die here, just like the prime minister.

"After another three weeks they finally let me go. I couldn't begin to guess at the amount of Uzbeks put out for the sake of a nice spread in our magazine."

Not all journalists are treated like such VIPs, of course. But they still receive preferential treatment, live in the best apartments, buy cars without waiting for five years, and get to go abroad. These are the wages for blabbering about sports, for diverting people whose thoughts might otherwise stray to questioning the moral values of Soviet society and asking why Soviet tanks were fired on in Rhodesia, what freedom of speech is, or how the party machinery operates.

SIX

Twenty Years and the Three-Second Payoff

The night of September 9, 1972: the Munich Basketball-halle watches the USSR edge out the United States 51–50 for its first basketball championship in Olympic history. The American media blast the victory as "highly disputable," "questionable," "controversial." One report leaves no room for doubt: the United States was "cheated out of the gold medal," it asserts. At the same time, a flourish of Russian papers trumpets a triumph: "a victory, fair and square"; "the razing of a monument"; "the inevitable collapse of the colossus"; "the breakdown of the American basketball machine."

The argument rages for five months between the U.S. officials, the jury of appeals of the International Amateur Basketball Association (FIBA), and a special commission of the IOC. The flare-up is fanned by irate letters from thousands of never-say-die Americans.

The American protest accuses the Russians of a time-out infraction: according to Article 41 of the FIBA rules, "A

coach has the right to request a charged time-out. He shall
do so by going in person to the scorer and asking clearly
for a time-out, making the proper conventional sign with
his hands. Electrical devices enabling coaches to request a
time-out without leaving their places may be used. The
scorer shall indicate to the officials that a request for
charged time-out has been made by sounding his signal as
soon as the ball is dead and the game watch is stopped but
before the ball is again in play."

Both U.S. coach Hank Iba and Vladimir Kondrashin of
the USSR had a time-out button to activate a bulb and
buzzer on the scorers' table. When questioned by a reporter, Kondrashin swore he had pressed his button before
Doug Collins received the ball for his first free throw; the
Longines clock was stopped, and the ball was technically
dead. In other words, everything had been in accordance
with the rules.

Reporter: "Is it possible the signal wasn't working?"

Kondrashin: "It was working just fine. I saw a film of
the game at an IOC session in Geneva. Not a videotape;
a film, with every detail in living color, screened for the
commission they set up to look into the American complaint. Everyone who saw the film saw the bulb light up—
and the scorers nodding at me. The idiots, they wanted to
give me the time-out before the first free throw; of course
I refused."

A key to the subsequent chain of events lies in Kondrashin's last sentence. Once his signal reaches the scorers,
a coach has the right to choose his time-out either before
or immediately after the first free throw. Given the situation three seconds prior to the end of a game, any coach
with the least bit of common sense (and there's no reason

to knock Kondrashin, as far as basketball's concerned) is going to take the time out afterward, so as to gear his final plan of action according to whether the basket is made.

It can be assumed that the four West German scorers—citizens of a country where basketball lies buried toward the bottom of the Olympic hit parade—honestly assumed Kondrashin had turned down time-out altogether. Kondrashin, on the other hand, relying on the electronics and convinced that a nod of his head would be understood as intending the time-out for after the throw, never bothered to walk up to the scorers in person. According to Soviet Junior Coach Sergei Bashkin, "After Collins made the first basket, the scorers took their own sweet time before sounding the time-out. In the meantime, referee Renato Righetto gave the ball back to Collins. And that was that: the moment the referee returns the ball to the player, neither team has the right to call a time-out. I dashed over to the scorers' table and screamed, 'We called a time-out, dammit!' They immediately turned on the siren, but it was too late. Anybody who even heard the signal in the pandemonium that followed thought it was the end-of-game whistle. Luckily, FIBA Secretary General William Jones saw the whole thing and stood up for us."

It may or may not be that Dr. Jones of Great Britain favored the Russians or found himself bored with sixty-three consecutive U.S. Olympic victories.

It's possible that junior referee Artenik Arabadzhan of Bulgaria really hadn't noticed his Soviet brother Ivan Edeshko stepping over the out-of-bounds line while making his famous full-court pass.

It's not impossible that the harried Righetto of Brazil missed Aleksandr Belov charging James Forbes on his way to the basket in the final seconds.

It's conceivable that the FIBA jury, made up of a Hungarian, an Italian, a Puerto Rican, and a Cuban, leaned politically to the Soviets and felt no misgivings over the contestable points of the game, which set an Olympic record for errors.

Only one thing is incontrovertible: whether the score had stayed 50–49 in favor of the Americans, as it was before the three seconds, or 50–51, as it stood at the end, neither of the teams could be said to have held all the aces. It was a contest of equals, equipped with the most up-to-date technical and tactical artillery. In one more of a chain of psychological showdowns in the athletic arena, the United States—boasting an eighty-year basketball history, eighteen million players of all walks of life, and a hundred and fifty million spectators annually—was challenged soundly by the Soviet Union, a country where the game was built up on the same cold war keystone as the skyscraper or the Bomb: "To overcome the American imperialists on land, sea, and sky."

The 1952 Helsinki Olympics was the Soviet team's first encounter with American giants, such as the 6'10¼" Clyde Lovelette and the 6'11¾" Bob Kurland. The tallest of the Russians was Otar Korkiia, at 6'2¾".

The American Gullivers played low post, dunking ball after blistering ball as gales of laughter accompanied the Lilliputians' desperate efforts to outjump them for possession. Though the quality of their game was light-years behind the Americans, miraculously they salvaged second place. "The U.S. owes its success not so much to strategy or skill as to size," commented Tass.

The Helsinki clinker convinced the Sports Committee it was time for a new era in Soviet basketball—an era aimed at bringing America to its knees, an era in which there would be no room for anyone under 6'7". A nationwide roundup of tall teenagers was declared. Coaches were commissioned to pick them up on the streets and at the movies, in stores and in subway stations, and promise their height in gold for appearing on the courts.

Candidates meriting these monetary metrics proved to be few and far between, and researchers proceeded to investigate why Russia was ravaged with retarded growth. Some advanced an "acceleration" theory, according to which human growth is directly proportional to the pace of daily life. Since they run a rat race at a compulsive sprint, these Lysenkoists proposed, Americans enjoy the dubious compensation of sportsworthy size. More serious scientists suggested that a well-balanced diet, pure water, and the eradication of many infectious diseases had created conditions conducive to the production of giants in America.

While the theorists bandied the matter about, coaches tried out a few gangly godsends, who turned out to be as lazy as they were lanky and ate enough for an army: goldbricks indeed.

Of all the titans ferreted out in the fifties, only Uvais "Vasilii" Akhtaev and Janis "The Breadwinner" Kruminsh held up as lasting competitive material. The two stunned the specialists, not only with their strength, speed, and shooting but also with some rather staggering changes in height.

Although everyone is slightly taller in the morning than in the evening, since the body tends to settle during the course of the day and stretch during sleep, this is barely noticeable in someone under 5'8". In Akhtaev the difference was unmistakable, varying from 7'6½" to an incredible 7'9¼". Recruited by the Alma-Ata Burevestniks at a time when there wasn't a player over 6'4¾" in all eleven Soviet major league teams, Akhtaev became the bane of the entire alliance. The opposition—all five of them—resorted to an aggressive blocking and pressing defense that spared only Akhtaev, against whom any maneuver was all but hopeless.

One quixotic team even tried blocking the giant—by hoisting a player onto another's shoulders and advancing the pyramid against him. The judges were stumped: the rule books had never thought of *that* one.

Since no one had yet thought of the 30-second rule either, many of the teams froze the ball without even attempting to attack the Burevestnik basket. The scores looked like soccer: 5–3, 7–4, 6–2.

Other teams, fed up with the futility of fighting the giant, took to off-the-court combat, sending pre-game sorties to the locker room to steal his shorts, jersey, and size 16 sneakers. Akhtaev would put on his street clothes, take the heels off his shoes, and go out on the floor unfazed.

The sight of the well-built 350 pounds looming on the court triggered a chain reaction among scouts to woo the giant for weight lifting, wrestling, and hockey. Having seen him reach up effortlessly to block sky-high shots at the basket, the envoys of hockey groomed Ahktaev for goalkeeping. He passed the test. Heavily suited up, he settled in in front of the net like a bear before its den and covered every corner. Yet his true love was basketball. Despite his size, he displayed elegant technique and split-second reflexes.

Privately, however, Akhtaev felt like a freak, a pariah. People gawked and pointed at him on the street. On the road, the regulation hotel beds gave him no choice but to spend sleepless nights on the hard floor. Once a clerk at the post office scolded him for poking his childlike face over the top of her window to ask about his mail. "Don't be naughty, little boy," she scolded. "Get down off those stilts!" When the girl saw it wasn't a prank, she fainted dead away.

For solace, Akhtaev carried a newspaper photo in his wallet of a smiling nine-foot Englishman. Even on the court he worried about standing out.

Akhtaev's frustrated opponents retaliated on the sly for his size by pinching, poking, and punching at his legs and back. Though he didn't dare use his fists in return, he found consolation in stepping "inadvertently" on a tormentor's toes or boosting him onto the boards and refusing to take him down until he got an apology. But the man who seemed cruel on court spent his free time writing long letters to his mother, a little black-haired woman who lived in a remote mountain village.

The public image was different. When the giant Kruminsh was discovered in Latvia at the end of the fifties, Akhtaev jealously boomed, "I'll teach that bastard to go and play basketball!"

Unlike Akhtaev, Kruminsh's height, as such, never bothered him; he quietly endured the inevitable mockery and radiated good will. Where Akhtaev was mostly afraid of looking funny, Kruminsh was terrified of his own strength: at 7'5" and 360 pounds, a quick turnaround shot could mow down nearby players the way a helicopter propeller would a ground crew.

A successful lumberjack for whom felling century-old oaks was like snapping carrots, Kruminsh was talked into basketball at twenty-four. But the late starter quickly proved to be talented. He was kept on the National Team for fifteen years and earned himself the nickname "The Breadwinner" for his pivotal contribution to the silver at the Rome and Tokyo Olympics.

The presence of Akhtaev and Kruminsh forced their intramural rivals into tactical innovation in order to cope. Soviet basketball had basically gotten under way in the summer of 1939, when the Red Army "liberated" the Baltic: Lithuania and Latvia between them had won three European championships in the years before the war, playing a disciplined pattern offense with chesslike precision. Nothing was left to chance: this was solid, academic basketball.

Without a tradition behind them, the Russians paid close attention to their shotgun in-laws and began beating them before they could put a label on such fundamentals as feinting or setting a pick. They were a rugged, fast-breaking team of winners—outnumbering the defensive team at the basket or fiercely persistent in the most hopeless of situations. The strict, scientific style lost to a raging ad-lib.

After the war, Georgian basketball made its appearance as a temperamental Brazilian-like spectacle with typically faultless, aggressive ball control but an amazingly sloppy defense.

The Helsinki defeat grafted together the three branches of Soviet basketball—the Baltic, the Russian, and the Georgian—into a powerhouse hybrid of short but hard-driving anti-Akhtaev and anti-Kruminsh snipers drilled in long-range offensive rebounding and forced to run faster, jump higher, pass harder, and receive better. The attack moved away from the giants at the boards toward long shots from midcourt. Before long, a whole new 6'3"–6'7" generation grew up that could stake a 6′10″–7′5″ opposition on equal footing.

As in all Soviet sports, the Moscow Army Sports Club holds first place in major league basketball. The Army clubs in Riga and Kiev fall not far behind.

The Moscow club includes the 6′4¾″ Ivan Edeshko, author of the golden assist in Munich, and the 6′3¾″ Sergei Belov, a 20-pointer in the same game who's widely considered not only the team's driveshaft but its intellectual chassis as well. The club has nurtured Vladimir Andreev (7′1½″) and Vladimir Tkachenko (7′3″), known as "Soviet Americans" for their combination of height and know-how. Team coach Aleksandr Gomelskii, a hoary, diminutive man of Jewish origin, forces his thick-skulled superiors to swallow a diet spiced with experiment. Out of it, he has fashioned a well-oiled mechanism that seems not so much a team as a demonstration of postindustrial victory technology.

As in soccer or hockey, the masses support Army's perennial rival, Spartak—this time of Leningrad. Spartak's property numbers the powerful twenty-two-year-old Aleksandr Belov, who made the final basket in Munich and likes to flex his muscles off the court as well as on: once, when another driver scratched his beloved Zhiguli, he caught up to the culprit, dragged him out of his car, and knocked him forty paces. He was given three years' probation.

Spartak is coached by the very Vladimir Kondrashin who led the Soviet squad to victory in Munich. Although a good-natured character, Kondrashin believes firmly that redirected rage is a decisive factor in any sports victory and is not above sarcasm, when necessary, to rile his players.

Since Kondrashin's psychology is in fact less than fool-proof, his team offers its numerous fans an odd mixture of eye-pleasing, heartwarming play and frequent maulings by the Army machine.

Riga, the capital of the Latvian Republic, is the home of the VEF team, which supposedly produces excellent radios and stereos when not on court, and the TTT, an athletic outlet for local female tram and trolley workers.

Voroshilovgrad, where not a single truck or car is produced, is the home of the Avtomobilists, who—like so much else in Soviet sports—owe their existence to the athletics-obsessed former provincial party secretary Vladimir Shevchenko.

There is a Dynamo team in Tbilisi, the capital of Soviet Georgia, and Frunze Burevestnik, the pride of the Kirghiz Republic, draws mobs of a whole two hundred—most of whom have just arrived by camelback.

In terms of popularity, basketball is clearly the stepchild of Soviet sports and consistently given the short end of the publicity stick. Except for the politically potent U.S. tourneys, the games are almost never broadcast on national TV. Gyms are small and dark, and the lavish sports palaces prefer booking big-box-office bands.

The statistics that claim some four million regular players most likely include any teenager who ever criss-crossed a court for phys. ed., scholarship collegians who play to get through school, and factory workers who dribble for their GTO.

Professional major league players are profiled in game reports, which the Sports Committee reviews when drafting athletes deserving the $350 monthly that comes with membership on the National Team. In addition to age, height, and weight, the dossiers include the following: who played, and for how many minutes; field goals made and free throws made and missed; rebounds grabbed; number of turnovers, violations, and personal fouls; total points scored.

Knowing that the average age of the best Olympic Americans is twenty-two, the officials seem concerned above all with how old a player is. Somehow they forget that Americans start as young as eight; their own players are rarely introduced to the game before fifteen, and peak, accordingly, at twenty-nine.

The officials compute the ratio of baskets to shots, recoveries to misses, and passes received to passes attempted. The mile-long résumés are then spread out over the floors of the Sports Committee building for review. The fate of a future member of the National Team is often decided without the player ever being seen in action.

The players, in turn, knowing all too well of this athletic algebra, risk nothing that might mar their profiles. They'd rather pass up a possible basket than "ruin their percentage," so they toss the ball to the nearest teammate.

Judging by his papers alone, Central Army's 5′8½″ Armenak Alachachian wouldn't have been worth the time of day. Though a superscorer when he tried, Alachachian was reluctant to shoot and limited himself to assisting his taller teammates. Thus, eyewitness raves over his technique at National Team training camps had no effect on his chances of going to the Olympics: he wasn't even suggested for the substitutes' bench.

Then, unexpectedly, Alachachian was asked to play against the Americans. Nervous, he lost the ball three times in the course of minutes, and the Russians lost the game.

One of the leaders of the Sports Committee stepped into the locker room afterward.

"He was fuming," Alachachian wrote later on. "He pushed past me and made a beeline for the coach. 'The Americans were pressing,' he said. 'Why the hell did you put that midget in? I never want to see him on the National Team again.'"

The episode persuaded Alachachian to throw in the towel for good, but he began longing for the game after only a month. Training again, he worked out a stunning piece of hocus-pocus. Whereas before he had had only two alternatives after dribbling—to pass or to shoot—now he found a third: an assist from an intentional rebound to himself. The combination relied on the element of surprise: all five players of the opposing team instinctively watched the ball head toward the boards and momentarily let him out of sight, winning him the split second he needed to get the ball back and transfer it to a predetermined, wide-open teammate. When he was used against the U.S. again in 1964 his two-step brought down the house, and the Americans with it. Coach John McLendon called him the best player in the game and added that even the Celtics would be glad to sign him.

The American's appraisal signaled V-Day against the Sports Committee paper war. Alachachian took a secure place on the National Team, played brilliantly at the Tokyo Olympics, and stayed with the major league until he was thirty-nine.

In 1971, as coach of the Army Club, Alachachian published *Basketball, Etcetera*, in which he wrote, "If I had my way I'd have a monument to coaches erected with the following words chiseled on it: 'Everything Soviet sports is today it owes to the coach.' And I'd make sure they put it where it could be seen from the committee chairman's window."

Alachachian goes on to describe the circumstances, more or less typical for any Soviet sport, surrounding his team's preparation for the European Cup against Réal of Madrid —which it lost by 17 points: "We started on the path to defeat long before ever going out on the courts. The defeat began in Moscow. There was one meeting after another where they told us we were the first Soviet athletes ever to go to Franco Spain, reminded us that the whole country would be watching us, impressed on us that everyone was counting on us not to disgrace the motherland, assured us that everyone believed in us, asked us whether we'd be worthy of their trust, entreated us to fight like men, and asked us how they could help.

"I don't doubt for a second that the intentions of the prime movers of the meetings were the highest; every one of them wished us well. But what they *did* do flagrantly contradicted what they *intended* to do.

"When we returned to Moscow (down by seventeen points but assured a return game at home), they upped the number of meetings dramatically. Some of them criticized us, some supported us, some asked us to give our all in the return game, others told us not to worry. Still others proposed plays we should run to recoup the points. Again they all wished us well—and interfered with our really getting ready for the game. At the next meeting—the tenth straight, I believe—I couldn't hold out any longer. When they asked what we needed for a victory in Moscow, I answered, plain and simple: 'No more of these goddamn meetings!' "

In 1974, at the height of his coaching career, Alachachian unexpectedly (or perhaps predictably, come to think of it) applied to reunite with his relatives in Toronto. The answer came back affirmative.

The single tradition in basketball is that it has no traditions. The theme of changeability was probably fated from its very founding in 1891 by James Naismith, an instructor at the Y.M.C.A. College in Springfield, Massachusetts.

"For goals I wanted two boxes eighteen inches square," Naismith once said, "but Mr. Stebbing, the janitor, couldn't find any. He did locate these two peach baskets here in the storeroom." Naismith compromised and the game was born. At first he prescribed seven players to a team; later, somebody decided nine would do better, which, after some years, they cut to eight. Today there are five.

In the early 1950s basketball was gangrenous with freezing the ball. Spectators were dying of boredom. A 30-second time limit put life into the game. Then being in the free-throw lane more than three seconds was prohibited, and blocking a field goal on the downward arc was forbidden. The zone-play rule was changed and then changed back again, the foul rule for the last three minutes was changed to five minutes and then, redesigned, back to three; the four-foul disqualification was increased to five. Rule-change fever reached such enormous proportions that the FIBA passed a resolution allowing new rules only once in eight years.

With or without new rules, the quality of the game has changed. Both Soviet and American teams have been engineered as sports machines to play supersonic basketball: one or two lightning passes end in taking the basket. Basketball as a performance of brilliant soloists with a diverse offensive repertoire has given way to a team-play chorus whose harmonious, if not monotonous, song is orchestrated by the coach.

And what about the millions of fans who enjoy a virtuoso show? Who knows? Sooner or later, tradition being what it is, Siberian Naismiths may emerge and teach boys from Nebraska to tilt the machine with a new and unbeatable basketball baroque.

SEVEN

Get That Gold!

In 1958, when figure skaters Stanislav and Nina Zhuk went all out with a two-and-a-half-turns Axel, they were taken to task for making a Punch-and-Judy show of *patinage artistique*. Preoccupied with elegance and musicality, purity of line and unity of composition, the figure-skating establishment wanted no part of the young innovators' astounding acrobatics. The best the Zhuks managed in world championships was a silver medal, and they bagged their single bronze by only a narrow margin. Even Soviet judges were wary of their "unseemly" style.

Ten years later, though Zhuk had traded in the performer's glitter for a trainer's tweed, his skating notions remained unchanged: he tutored Irina Rodnina and Aleksei Ulanov to fly through the air in a manner less fitting for a rink than for a gym. What was more, the words he sent flying found as little favor as his pedagogical freethinking. He called two-time Olympic champions Liudmila Belousova and Oleg Protopopov hopelessly old-fashioned, pronounced their ever-dying swan at long last dead, and suggested they'd do better clearing the hell out of competition altogether. Alone among the coaches of the National Team, Zhuk had the temerity to take potshots at his prizewinning peers, refusing to concede that their methods were just as valid as his own.

In the Soviet Union the seriousness of the reaction to this sort of barrage depends less on the content of the criticism than on the assailant's connections: an uncle on the Central Committee, a cousin in some ministry, or a father-in-law with the joint chiefs of staff. Over many a midnight supper, Zhuk's victims began poking among the branches of his family tree. As soon as it was plain he had nothing behind him but conviction and candor—qualities that left him as impotent as a king without his crown—the outraged opposition started honing the blades of revenge.

Next to *Pravda* and *Izvestiia*, the biggest newspaper in the Soviet Union is *Komsomolskaia Pravda* (circulation, twelve million). Like the others, it proceeds not from the premise of "all the news that's fit to print" but from all the codes that fit the purposes of its politics. The fifty-three-year-old *Komsomolskaia Pravda*, the official organ of the Communist Youth League, was founded with the aim of "rooting out the vestiges of a bourgeois yesterday"—and guarding youngsters against the West's tempting cornucopia today. The paper's censorious tone has more than once been called downright venomous.

Articles and letters published in the paper have been known to precipitate party committee investigations, and the consequences have sometimes been tragic. In 1937 my father, deputy rector of Dnepropetrovsk University, was arrested after *Komsomolskaia Pravda* published a letter they entitled "The Blight of Liberalism." He was given ten years for his alleged Trotskyite activities, which the letter had taken pains to detail. He died in a labor camp, to be rehabilitated posthumously after twenty years. In the late forties, *Komsomolskaia Pravda* constituted the shock troops in the campaign against "cosmopolitanism," leading to the imprisonment of countless Jewish intellectuals.

In more recent years, while the paper's tone remains no less venomous, at least its pronouncements no longer lead to mass arrest. Labor camps have been replaced by public shaming or the destruction of a career. The newspaper informs the masses of the outcome of its attacks on their degenerate comrades with a few crisp lines in a column called "The Measures Taken." And, if the editors find the measures taken insufficient, they throw a few more punches.

In 1963 the paper published an article by Vladimir Soloukhin in which Fëdor Solianik, the head of the Soviet whaling industry—a Hero of Socialist Labor and the time-honored idol of millions—was denounced as a petty dictator and a general good-for-nothing. Such a lunge at a lionized personality would never see print in *Pravda* or *Izvestiia*, which passes along the government line through a claque of conservative editorial Cossacks. But *Komsomolskaia Pravda* usually either gets away with its iconoclasm or falls back on the leniency shown youthful impertinence the world over. In the case of Solianik, Yuri Voronin, editor in chief at the time, had simply been unaware that the bureaucrat and Nikita Khrushchev were old drinking buddies, and the information gap cost him his post. A year later Leonid Brezhnev encouraged the abashed editorial board to bare its teeth once more.

It is not only against individuals that *Komsomolskaia*

Pravda crusades, but against various Soviet institutions: factories resorting to illegal production gimmicks, universities not worthy of the name, and ministries remiss in their "socialist obligations."

Since 1970 the last page of the four-page daily has been given over entirely to sports: it was finally recognized that the younger generation was having trouble downing Leninist dogma without laughing and neither trusted nor took interest in anything but athletics. The paper made it known that the stadium was the place where a youngster could now comfortably display his or her patriotism, heroism, collective consciousness, and moral fortitude.

There is hardly a single Soviet sports star who has escaped the klieg lights of *Komsomolskaia Pravda*. Having the conviction (and events having supported it) that champions are more susceptible than most to corruption and more difficult to fetter with prescriptions for behavior, the editors praise the stars with great caution—just in case they someday have to cut them down to size.

In contrast to *Sovetskii Sport*—published by the Sports Committee with minimal controversy in order to promote the impression that all is well under its auspices—*Komsomolskaia Pravda* has been known to tell the committee itself where to get off. Amid the usual welter of ideological cliché, which every practiced reader ignores as if by instinct, the paper's spicier stories—though rare—have given *Komsomolskaia Pravda* a newsy reputation; subscribers turn to the last page for sparks of excitement the way they do to page one in the West.

The following letter, headed "They're Getting Away with Murder" and signed by six leading coaches of the national figure skating team, appeared in the November 16, 1968, issue:

Dear Editor:

We are writing to the Komsomol paper because what we have to say has to do with the upbringing of young athletes. Let's start by mentioning just one episode, which, unfortunately, did not fail to slip past millions of TV viewers at the Grenoble Olympics. Remember the wonderful moment when our "Golden Pair" of figure skating, two-time Olympic champions Liudmila Belousova and Oleg Protopopov, were greeted by an ovation as they stood on the highest step of the winners' platform? It seems only one pair of athletes, a mere step below, "forgot" to congratulate them. Only so as not to provide silage for sensation-seeking Western papers did the champions finally shake the hands of their rival teammates. But we will not reproach these athletes, for "There are no bad students—only bad teachers."

Let us now turn our attention to the tutor of the Silver Pair—Honored Coach of the Soviet Union, Honored Master of Sport, Comrade Stanislav Zhuk. There he stood, arms folded, right in front of the TV cameras. Millions saw how he turned his back as Belousova and Protopopov entered. To an outsider this might have seemed just chance, an unfortunate slip, but we know better: we know all too well of those interviews he has so zealously been granting foreign columnists, and we know that what he did to the Golden Pair was, alas, hardly accidental.

We have read those interviews in foreign publications, and we can testify that Zhuk continually expatiates on our champions' flaws while obsessively extolling his pair alone. Is this befitting for a Soviet coach?

The letter goes on to put forth additional instances of Zhuk's disgraceful behavior:

We dare not cite most of the language Zhuk uses with his colleagues. But we submit just one, barely printable, example, addressed to Honored Coach of the Soviet Union

Tatiana Tolmachëva, an individual respected by all sportsmen: "Just wait, I'll drown you like a mangy kitten in a slop
pail!" This because Comrade Tolmachëva, a judge at the
competition, consigned his pupils to second place.

One of Zhuk's "teaching methods" is to collect personal
vouchers from his charges saying he's the one that taught
them a particular technique. He keeps the vouchers in his
tweed jacket, and every time his students win he shakes the
papers in his fist as proof he's the one to thank for it.

For some reason—whether out of fear or mesmerized by
his past performance—there's no one who's yet had the
nerve to straighten him out.

The letter closed by calling upon the Soviet sports community to rid itself of an element scornful of its noble
principles. The signers included senior coach of the
National Team Viacheslav Zaitsev and honored coaches of
the Soviet Union Elena Chaikovskaia, Igor Moskvin, and
Tatiana Tolmachëva.

Despite this united outburst of indignation, it would be
a mistake to assume the least unanimity among the above-
named. Quite the contrary. Every one of them has his or
her own school of skating and works behind closed doors
—deeply convinced of his or her own system's superiority
while pathologically jealous of the innovations of the
others. Their relationships become most aggravated at
National Team recruiting time, when each is fighting
desperately to have his disciples numbered among the
selectees. It happened that when the National Team began
readying for Grenoble, several of these disciples defected
to Zhuk, later sharing their honor with him as they
ascended the winners' platform. Such maneuvers were
clearly less than endearing to their former teachers.

Grenoble gold medalists Belousova and Protopopov, on

the other hand, had worked out their own training programs and wanted nothing to do with the whole lot of Soviet coaches. "Nor will we ever *become* coaches," asserted Protopopov. "Skaters of our caliber can't be cultivated, and we're not going to stoop to manufacturing mediocrities, like everyone else around."

The free-style composition on ice begins with a quest for appropriate music. A skater is no less an interpreter of Wagner or Chopin on the ice rink than is a violinist on the concert stage: the violinist explores the music's shadings with his bow, while the skater interprets the melodies with the blades of his skates—gliding lightly along the ice or stinging it like a wasp, stroking it like a cat's paw, or spinning on it like a top. For a five-minute program, a pair and their coach attempt to meld two or three taped compositions that join andantes, adagios, and allegros smoothly into a single coherent piece.

Once the audio part is settled upon, they work out its visual expression: progressives, spins, swings, jumps, and connecting movements. A single five-minute program can involve as many as thirty elements, some of enormous physical difficulty. Properly selected music underscores each movement in a way that enhances its impression immeasurably.

On the other hand, taking the music in segments too small is destructive to the melodic line. Worse, the stunts seem to exist independent both of each other and of the music, which sounds as though it had been written by a computer suffering high fever.

In the early sixties, Belousova and Protopopov decided not to fuse disparate musical compositions but to devote the entire five minutes to illuminating the poetic images of a single piece by Liszt, Tchaikovsky, Beethoven, Massenet, or Rachmaninoff: the first flutter of young love, the ecstasy of fulfillment, the unforeseen storm, the sorrow of breaking up, the relationship remembered.

Liudmila is a graceful blonde, clear-headed and self-possessed, with a contemplative demeanor and a soft smile. Oleg is tall and thin, nervous and compulsive. Liudmila's warmheartedness underlines the lyricism of their routines; Oleg's stormy temperament supports the rhythm and dynamics.

In order to give the music more complex expression, the pair rejected conventional shadow skating, in which the male partner's movements parallel the woman's. They expanded the performing area, counterpoising each other's motions at opposite corners of the rink. This counterpoint was accentuated by finely metrical gesture and mime.

The pair learned to glide along the ice with such weightlessness, delicacy, and precision that their skating was described as "soundless"—unlike the grating style of others that sent ice powder flying up from under the blades. They perfected the death spiral, with Liudmila revolving three times at the center of the rink, back arched, head nearly touching the ice.

The champions' interpretation of Massenet's "Méditation" and Saint-Saëns' "Dying Swan" had an impact more powerful than their counterparts in ballet did onstage: where dancers must break their pace at the point of greatest strain for an arbitrary turn into the next position, skaters are in continuous motion. And it is precisely this breathtaking fluidity that never fails to thrill TV audiences, at which figure skating is mainly aimed.

No skaters even came close to Belousova and Protopopov between 1962, when they first won the world championship, and 1968, when they captured their second Olympic gold. In 1969 Oleg turned thirty-six and Liudmila thirty-four: knowing they had no chance against competitors on the basis of soul-stirring stunts or lightning speed, the champions advanced an "artistic" theory of skating incorporating French *patinage artistique* and German-style *Eiskunstlauf*. They announced the style as beyond the reach of other skaters, who, "failing to express the richness of a composition, try instead to darn their musical holes with a jump here and a lift there."

The two were counting on another factor as well. Figure-skating judges are more cautious and conservative than in any other sport. Though from different countries and often with different points of view, these nine men and women have sat alongside one another for years and are agreed upon one thing: they will do everything possible to uphold the status quo, to the point of granting high scores to flawed performances by old champions before acknowledging the value of brash new contenders. It takes a revolutionary, incontrovertibly impressive performance before they will yield first place to a newcomer. At the beginning of the 1969 season there was nothing to indicate that a revolutionary pair of the kind would appear on the scene.

Figure skating is the only sport that even compares with soccer in its drawing power for the Soviet citizenry. In January, February, and March—the peak of the season—Russians glue themselves to their TV screens in blockbusting numbers: media researchers report something like 125 million viewers the night of the European or world championships. The Russian people have always loved music and dance; their enjoyment is intensified when these elements are blended with the simple but dazzling movements of figure skating. All other forms of entertainment are eclipsed, while parents sit pointing at the screen, instructing their children to follow the champions' example.

The harsh fact, however, is that to be admitted to a skating school is more difficult than to pass the entrance exams at Moscow University. First, there are few such schools. Most of these, located in Moscow and Leningrad, enjoy a cachet comparable to that of the most exclusive of Connecticut's country clubs. Even the bureaucrats admit that the mass approach seen in other Soviet sports is absent in figure skating, if only because of the limited availability of artificial ice. More important, countless hours of work with a large group of specialists are demanded for every pair of world-class youngsters.

But the glimmer of the sports star, reaching into overcrowded living rooms, inspires the drive to be a winner. Only a few make it; thousands fail. Yet *Komsomolskaia Pravda* is flooded with inquiries about the route to stardom. Other letters wax lyrical over the beauty of their compatriots' performances. If nothing else, the "letters to the editor" column serves the same purpose as the podium at the plant auditorium: letting your comrades know you're involved in public activity. Should the mail deviate from the desirable, *Komsomolskaia Pravda* doctors it according to a tried-and-true recipe: 99.99 percent in support of the previous paper's statements, .01 percent dissenting from it.

In the case of a controversial issue, such as that of Zhuk, the overwhelming popular anger that followed the coaches' letter clearly signaled the beginning of a showdown. The sentiment of the Sports Committee, however, was unanimous: Zhuk would not be thrown to the dogs, and a silence would be maintained. Yet to opt for silence of any duration would only end in the sports executives themselves being kicked by the paper for the cover-up. The minutes of a committee session was dispatched to "The Measures Taken" column disclosing that "Comrade Zhuk has been given a stern dressing down. The appropriate notation has been made in his personal file."

Zhuk's enemies didn't buy the story. Meanwhile, after a training session of the National Team at a suburban Moscow dacha, the angry Zhuk decided to get even. He packed his skaters onto a bus, waited until Belousova and Protopopov showed up, promptly slammed the door in their faces, and ordered the driver to step on the gas. The Golden Pair was left stranded twenty miles outside the city.

The next day Belousova and Protopopov blew into the offices of *Komsomolskaia Pravda* brandishing two points. First, Zhuk had borne them a personal grudge ever since the 1950s, when they were training under rival theorist Pëtr Orlov. He continually made disparaging remarks to them, talked about them behind their backs, and ultimately had them expelled. What he was doing now was no different: conspiring to turn the Sports Committee against them. Second, Zhuk was having his pupils imitate Canadians Barbara Wagner and Robert Paul while dismissing the achievements of the native Russian school, for which Belousova and Protopopov had paved the way.

Did they really believe what they were saying? Hardly, under the circumstances: both were intelligent and pro-Western. But finding themselves isolated and under fire, they had lost their heads and launched a sneak counterattack behind the lines of cheap, but ever effective, Soviet soapboxing.

That was all it took. *Komsomolskaia Pravda* deputy editor Mikhail Blatin began preparing a piece called

"They're Getting Away with It Yet Again." Having gotten wind of the paper's intention, sports executives began making dozens of phone calls and lunch invitations entreating the newspaper to hold its peace. They swore that a conspiracy was entirely imaginary and that Zhuk, however eccentric a personality, would be the only man able to train new world-class pairs once Belousova and Protopopov slipped from their golden status—which would surely be in no more than another year.

Nothing helped. The article appeared on January 8, 1969, just days before the European championships, demanding in no uncertain terms that Zhuk be sacrificed for the sake of "educating youth in the spirit of gentility and good breeding, to appreciate not only the beauty of movement but also the beauty of getting along with one's fellows."

The Sports Committee was forced to remove Zhuk as National Team coach, and his pupils Irina Rodnina, nineteen, and Aleksei Ulanov, twenty-one, went to Garmisch-Partenkirchen without him. The two astonished their rivals, the judges, and the spectators with five minutes of uninterrupted stunts, each more complicated than the one before. Their trouncing of Belousova and Protopopov elicited ecstatic approbation from the overseas media: "dazzling spectacle"; "an inexhaustible fountain of energy"; "super-complex, cosmically ultra-modern skating."

A press conference followed on the heels of the victory.

Reporter: "Belousova and Protopopov think of figure skating as an art rather than a sport. How do you feel?"

Irina Rodnina: "The former champions have a thirty-second segment in which Protopopov draws Belousova to him and releases her three times in a row, holding her by the fingers. This comes off rather pretty when they do it, I suppose. But let's face it, it's ballet."

Aleksei Ulanov: "Right—ballet. But figure skating isn't ballet on ice. It's a sport—and, I think, a sport for the young. It's rare you'll find a really top figure skater over twenty-five these days."

Reporter: "And how do you feel about your performance being criticized for lacking their lyricism?"

Irina Rodnina: "It's true we don't show the depth of feeling they do, but tell me—I'm only nineteen, so why should I try to play with a kind of experience I haven't yet had and they have? I can't—and, what's more, I don't want to—come off like some *artiste*. But I do have something of my own to offer. If Aleksei and I started imitating them, we'd never have won. Coach Zhuk found a style that was right for *us*—and it's just the opposite of theirs, which I think everybody's bored with by now anyway."

Stanislav Zhuk has the square jaw and flattened snout of a bulldog and exercises a bulldog's grip in his work. But his eyes—sometimes tired, more often vital—add considerable humanity to his austere appearance. Referring to himself as a Stanislavskian on ice, his byword is "Beauty in complexity."

Though his manners differ from Stanislavsky's no less than a peasant's boots from the slippers of a prince, Zhuk is a match for the great director in trouncing anyone going after his turf.

The Moscow Army Sports Club had one of the best skating complexes in the world built for him. In addition to the main training rink, it houses a dance floor and recording studio, a movie theater and cable TV, a medical office and a needle bath, a swimming pool, and even a beauty parlor. Staffing these facilities under Zhuk's supervision is a small army of professionals, including audio-visual specialists, choreographers, music arrangers, costume designers, and physicians.

Only teenagers who have already shown their mettle elsewhere as beginning skaters are considered for admission. Zhuk believes twelve, thirteen, or fourteen to be the optimum age at which to begin working with girls, and fifteen, sixteen, or seventeen with boys.

He begins the creation of a future pair by selecting the female partner. Then he begins his search for the male—usually a boy ten to fifteen inches taller and fifty to sixty pounds heavier than the girl, with obvious native ability. The prospective pair next attempts a piece together. Zhuk considers any failures in harmony unimportant; rather, he looks at the ice for how the duo traces the figures he will eventually want to build.

Having decided on the pair, he begins training them away from the Army complex. First he teaches his pupils literally how to walk. Whatever their age, on the sidewalk or in a park, he watches how they move and has them push consciously off the ground in ways that will develop specific groups of leg muscles.

Since the boy and girl rarely exhibit identical physical qualities—he might be a good jumper but weak in the arms, while she might be poor at jumping but strong in stamina—Zhuk works on developing personalized sets of exercises—calisthenics, dumbbells, and even ball games—to balance their skills more equally. It is at this stage that he attends to the development of the back, arm, and abdominal muscles.

During the initial three or four months he allows the pair onto the rink only for a game of ice hockey—his object being to introduce them to the need for quick reflexes and courage and to make them feel at home on the ice in every way. In time the boys and girls become adept enough to manage fore-checking and slap shots against power-play teams. Although she was already a figure-skating champion, Irina Rodnina played hockey at every training session, and with such abandon that she was once hit in the face by a hundred-mile-an-hour puck. For weeks neither Max Factor nor Red Moscow makeup were of any avail in disguising the black-and-blue of her nose.

Following the nets and pucks stage, Zhuk at last allows each partner onto the ice for figure-skating training. After a five- to fifteen-minute warmup, he coaches the boy in stroking, spinning, and striking poses, while the girl watches from the bench. For two hours, three times a week, the boy and girl go out alternately without once skating together. They spend the other three days of the six-day training week on intensive gym and pool work. This goes on for five to seven months, during which the coach matches the skaters' innate talents to their early skills.

After a year the boy and girl are ready to skate as a pair. Zhuk has defined eight stages in mastering pairs skating:

1. Forward and backward progressives around the rink, holding each other hand in hand or hand on waist while keeping up the same stroke and thrust.

2. Shadow skating: separate but synchronous forward and backward progressives.

3. Spins and spirals, in which the boy swings his partner around his axis by the hand or waist. These maneuvers range from simple pirouettes to death spirals, but Zhuk

relegates them—once the backbone of the free-skating program—to the status of mere connecting elements, used only to hold the program together.

4. Rhythmic variation: the same step can be done to diverse times, from one-two, to waltz, to rock-'n'-roll.

5. The gems of the program—ultracomplex lifts and pair jumps. The great jumps are distinguished according to the part of the blade from which they are made—forward or back, inside or outside—and named after the skaters who created them: Axel, Salchow, Rittberger, Lutz. Zhuk fused these European standards with his Russian acrobatics to produce spectacular, thoroughly original stunts.

An important detail at this stage is learning to sustain a smile through even the most difficult moments of the program—five minutes of which, in terms of physical and nervous energy, equals a 5,000-meter race. After beaming with uninterrupted bliss on the rink, skaters will occasionally faint or burst into tears of relief the moment they return to the privacy of the locker room.

6. Music work, in which the pair and their coach collaborate with a composer or arranger. Zhuk prefers five or six melodies of contrasting mood, rhythm, and tempo per program, knowing that to show off their sophisticated acrobatics the pair needs a wide spectrum of musical accompaniment.

7. Choreographic refinements. Once the program is understood in principle, Zhuk invites a choreographer to work out the gestures, poses, and pauses. But he makes it known at the outset that he wants nothing to do with the guiding principles of classical stage ballet. His most complicated stunts are here transformed from unconnected kaleidoscopic mechanics into subtle internal dialogue.

8. Putting the final touches to the program, blending its individual parts to perfection. Section by section, they polish the piece until it is radiantly ready for competition.

Though these basic stages are fixed, Zhuk adapts them to the individual needs of the pair. But never for a moment, in years of training, has he withdrawn his iron hand, monitoring every facet of his students' lives and demanding that they record every thought, every reaction on the ice in a diary ready for regular presentation. By thus nosing out their moods and emotions, he manipulates even their psychological strengths and weaknesses in the service of their art.

And his control does not stop here. He specifies the girl's décolletage and the boy's jacket color. He ordains the allowable haircut and inspects pins, belts, and sleeves. He has concocted anthropometrical schemes that coordinate costumes to the body's dimensions and the program's demands. Zhuk is indeed a dictator, but there are tens of thousands of Russian youngsters who'd give anything to lay themselves at his feet.

Only at official championships—five minutes, after years of training—does Zhuk turn his gaze from his wards: he knows it is vital they be neither inhibited nor distracted by his facial expression, which till now has been arbiter of their universe. Only the roar of the crowd will make him look at them, as a smile of approval crosses his face.

It is nine years since Irina Rodnina has held first place in world championships and the Olympics—a record surpassed so far only by ten-time champion Sonja Henie—and there seems to be no stopping her. Among the judges, there has been no question of where the gold was to go;

they have been freed to busy themselves with assigning the silver and bronze.

At twenty-seven, Irina today has the same impish haircut and the same youthful, Zhuk-trained gait as at eighteen. But her tomboyish brashness has been tempered by the years, by reflection and experience, and her hazel eyes show less of their former sparkle.

In a recent interview, after being awarded the Order of Lenin, she commented that what she now values most is honesty. And ever honest with herself, she realizes she has begun to tire of her skating style and feels the time has come at last for lyricism—that same emphasis on intensity of feeling for which she once so vehemently criticized Belousova and Protopopov. The search for a means to express her new maturity on ice is a formidable one, but she is determined to find it—and, once it is found and implemented, to retire undefeated. Uncompromising with herself, she expects mirrorlike excellence from her partners —a germ of despotism she has picked up from Zhuk.

When her new partner, Aleksandr Zaitsev, slipped up for an instant at the Innsbruck Olympics, Rodnina cast him a glance that could have blasted Hiroshima. But after the performance she lay her head almost contritely on his shoulder and sniffled for a handkerchief to dry her eyes.

With Aleksei Ulanov, the man with whom she began her triumphal career, things were different. Although he was sometimes worthy of respect as a partner, more often he deserved the acute parody at which she was a master.

Ulanov grew up under his mother's wing. It was his mother who first shepherded him to the rink, and when he was admitted to Zhuk's school she launched an elaborate campaign to involve herself in the program, finally forcing the coach to give her a hand in the boy's training: he let her come to workouts and even took her along to out-of-town competitions.

At the same time, in order to ensure her son a future place in Moscow's jet set, she wangled his admission into the Gnesin Music School, one of the nation's most prestigious. But he studied neither Bach's fugues on the piano nor Rachmaninoff's romances on the violin. Ulanov was introduced to the bayan (the Russian folk accordion), *de rigueur* in Gnesin's contribution to the party line on the return to national roots in contemporary Soviet music.

Before Ulanov arrived each day at the rink, there was nothing Irina enjoyed more than to gather her schoolmates to caricature the boy skating with the bayan in his hands, his mother conducting alongside with a shrill vocal arpeggio.

Irina's parents, unlike Ulanov's, had brought her up in a manner reminiscent of the sink-or-swim child-rearing practices of American Indians. Having contracted tuberculosis at one and a half, she was put through a regime to strengthen her health: her parents took her walking for five or six hours at a time, year after year, in the minus-forty Russian winter; they had her jump in the snow, play with it, wash her face with it.

Not only did Irina survive; she became uncommonly rugged. From the day the five-year-old began skating, she worked determinedly at besting her friends. As an adult, she proved continually that she could outjump and outrace Ulanov. This did not distress Ulanov; what did disturb him was her lack of romantic interest. In 1972, if only to recover his pride, he began dating Liudmila Smirnova—who, with her partner, Andrei Suraikin, had held second place for years in the world pairs hierarchy.

Tall, kindhearted Liudmila had never learned to say

nyet, and she responded to Ulanov's advances only so as not to hurt his feelings. But time worked its magic, and an affair begun casually blossomed into wholehearted love.

The situation became explosive. Irina, daily eyeing the billing and cooing of the lovers, sensed that she was losing contact with her partner. As Ulanov continued showing off like a victorious bull, Irina—though never clearly resentful—realized that their partnership had been ruined. Her disappointment softened her mien, and her face began to betray traces of uncertainty. But this didn't last long: she decided to call it quits with Ulanov.

Neither Zhuk's strong-arm approach nor Sports Committee chairman Pavlov's personal entreaties—heavily laced with lyrics about the irreparable loss the motherland would suffer by the separation—swayed her in the least. Irina held her tongue. Her silence was more eloquent than words.

Ten months before the 1973 European championships, Zhuk issued an SOS for partners to every figure-skating school in the USSR. Candidates turned up by the hundreds. Only Zhuk's nose for talent could ever have divined the ideal partner for Rodnina in Zaitsev, an amateur weekend skater he had spotted in a Leningrad park.

Although Zhuk's primary criteria were satisfied—Zaitsev was 6'2" and 180 pounds—his choice was based more on the gentleness, intelligence, and subtlety he saw in the skater, qualities badly needed to douse Irina's hotheaded disposition. The coach knew that Rodnina would die rather than allow herself to hurt him.

Two months into training them together, Zhuk saw the first signs of rapport in the pair: not only wasn't Irina mocking her new partner, but she watched him with uncharacteristic diffidence.

Six months later, to finish synchronizing their physical skills, Zhuk sent the pair off alone to a summer camp on the Black Sea. By the time they returned to regular training at the Moscow complex their performance had improved considerably, synchronized by a full-blown romance. The two became European and world champions— and man and wife. The wedding was aired on national TV. And, in the quick succession of a slapstick routine, Ulanov married Smirnova and slipped to the silver step on the winner's platform.

Although Belousova and Protopopov spent the next few years in all-out war against the newcomers by grafting their younger rivals' grandstand stunts onto their once-crowd-pleasing program, they failed to adjust. Yet, they disavowed their shortcomings and accused the judges of plotting against them. Finally they conceded the end of their days in competition and magisterially joined the Leningrad ice ballet (and later the Canadian ice revue—the first athletes the Soviet government has ever permitted to make a few bucks hard cash). As pros, Belousova and Protopopov have become world champions once again.

Two giants of coaching survive the squabbling and squawking that have dominated Soviet figure skating: Stanislav Zhuk and Elena Chaikovskaia. For strategic reasons, Zhuk has recently been transferred to training a younger generation of skaters, while Rodnina and Zaitsev have been taken over by Tatiana Tarasova, the inventive and inspired twenty-nine-year-old daughter of noted hockey coach Anatolii Tarasov.

The year 1976 saw the spectacular debut on international rinks of twelve-year-old Elena Vodorezova, who made short order of astounding three-turn jumps and stunts indistinguishable from those of the world's best adult male skaters John Curry and Toller Cranston. At the world championships in Tokyo just a year later she received top score for the free-skating program and junior's silver for overall performance—described by American coach Carlo Fassi as "captivatingly dynamic . . . the style of the future."

It is likely that there was only one man in that audience of thousands able to refrain from gaping at the rink. Yet, tweed-jacket collar tucked under the bulldog jaw, tired eyes cast downward at his shoes, he transformed every sound of the girl's skates into an image of unmistakable clarity. Suddenly he could hold back no longer, breaking his practice of many years. He raised his eyes and riveted them on Elena. His glower pierced the skater as his thoughts bubbled over in unpronounced phrases: What the hell is she doing? . . . Get up there! Somersault! No, no! Stupid brat! How many times have I told you not to move into a jump like that? Well . . . Dazzle those damned judges with that finale of yours! Ah . . . Ah! Shit . . . you snot-nose little dummy!

A couple of minutes later, smiling for the TV cameras, the man was down by the rink kissing the girl, straightening the light blue bows that stuck up from her hair like propellers: "Atta girl, Lenochka! You blew it here and there, but, dammit, you weren't half bad! *Molodets*! Next year we're gonna get that gold!"

EIGHT

○━○━━━━○━○

Tomorrow's Another Game

Moscow, Friday, September 23, 1972: the second half of the Team Canada–Team USSR hockey series had begun.

Bobby Clarke slashed savagely into Valerii Kharlamov's shin and Ron Ellis pummeled him like a punching bag. Gilbert Perreault sank his teeth into Boris Mikhailov's nose while Phil Esposito simulated a saber dance. Gary Bergman kicked the sprawling Evgenii Mishakov for all he was worth. J.P. Parise came shaking his fists after the referee, who faked back to the officials' table and swung around with a snicker: another step and he could have slapped the player with game misconduct. When Parise was later banished to the penalty box anyway, the Canadian bench showered the ice with a hail of chairs, maple-leaf buttons, and wet towels.

Leonid Brezhnev, Nikolai Podgornyi, and Aleksei Kosygin watched impassively from the government boxes as the home-team fans screamed at them to nuke the aggressors. Only the amazing upset—5–4, in favor of the Russians—averted World War III, and the citizens used up a month of the town's liquor reserve the same night to douse their fiery pride.

The tumult was unprecedented in Soviet sports, and the TV cameras steered clear of it; the overflow fifteen thousand jamming Luzhniki Sports Palace witnessed a commotion that the tens of millions on international hook-up missed.

And never had there been a bigger hullabaloo than before the hockey series. Tickets went to organizations and ministries, which handed them to the shock workers of Communism, the most active of party activists and the most reliable of government bureaucrats. Huge lines waited all night by campfires fed with dry sticks and autumn leaves on the off chance of picking up the few remaining $1.50 tickets by morning.

Tickets scalped by the black market at $25, $50, and $100 sold out on the spot. The bored cops seemed less concerned with harassing the hawkers than getting out of uniform and latching onto some of the goods themselves.

Some fifty thousand had converged on Luzhniki by the start of the first game. The columns of police, expecting an ordinary game, were caught unawares, and mounted reinforcements had difficulty making their way through the crowds to their posts. Nor did the mob disperse even after the game had begun; thousands stayed glued to their radios outside for over two hours without losing hope they'd break in for a glimpse of the final ten minutes.

After the game, inspired by the rinkside battle, fans on their way home pushed and elbowed their way into the nearest subway station. Moscow's model metro became a dirty free-for-all beyond a New Yorker's worst nightmare. No "Sorry" or "Excuse me"; just a quiet punch or kick, followed by a brief wallet check against pickpockets. With hands and legs immobilized in the cars, an accidental jab to the liver could still call forth a healthy spit in return.

Aboveground, on the relatively empty Luzhniki parking lot (there being one car for every thirty-two people in Moscow), a graying, heavy-set man with puffy jowls and a slightly hooked nose checked for his side-view mirror ($50 on the black market), opened the door, pulled the windshield wipers up from under the seat, and screwed them back on.

Driving home in his private Volga was the only privilege that remained to him. Through the whole game he had sat high up in an uncomfortable spot, occasionally recognized by his neighbors, who whispered and got up for a closer look. Panting, he'd pound his knee with his fist, then turn away from the game to reread his crumpled program and crumple it up again.

The man was perhaps the only one present who had dreamed about this occasion for twenty-five years. But he had more than dreamed: he had worked and prepared for it without letup. Just six months before, he couldn't have imagined that someone else would be leading the Russian squad to the games.

Nor could millions of Soviets, who had grown accustomed to his face on TV, a veritable reflection of the drama on ice: childlike joy at a dynamic attack, indignation hissed at an ineffective pass, a hearty Russian laugh at a sudden goal.

Fifty-seven-year-old Colonel Anatolii Tarasov, the most famous man in all of Soviet sports, a laureate of the nation's highest awards, former coach of the Central Army Club and National Team, not only had not been invited to the officials' stands but had been forced to procure a ticket, like fresh lobster or American cigarettes, through private connections.

How could the Canadians—the best professionals on ice and 3–0, 4–1 at the end of the first two periods—slip to 4–5 by the close of the third? The breaks? Then how had they lost the games 2–1–1 at home? Had Moscow sent spies to flash red signals behind their net?

Indeed, there had been an intelligence briefing, but no Communist conspiracy. According to Vladislav Tretiak, currently acclaimed the world's premier goalie, "An hour before the first Montreal game Jacques Plante, the famous 'puck tamer' and the best goalie in the history of North American hockey, paid us a visit in the locker room and went into great detail telling me how to handle Mahovlich, Esposito, Cournoyer, Henderson. 'Mahovlich shoots whenever and wherever he gets the puck,' he cautioned. 'Come out of the net to cut down on the angle. Keep in mind, Cournoyer's the fastest forward in the NHL and Dennis Hull can score from the red line.'

" 'Phil Esposito's the most dangerous player on the team: the guy'll score if you leave him the slightest opening. Just don't give him room to operate in the crease: once he's in, there's no defenseman in the world that can move him out.'

"Plante made it all more graphic on a blackboard, said good-bye, and left. We sat there dumbfounded. What was he trying to pull? Maybe he knew Esposito was getting ready to rip me to shreds and felt sorry for me: after all, I was only twenty. Maybe it was the brotherhood of goalies. I don't know . . . Only, his advice sure helped: we won seven–three.

"By the way, after the game they left the rink without shaking hands, despite championship tradition. At first we were ticked off, but then we realized pros never do. If I win, they figure, it's money out of my rival's pocket, so why the hell should he want to shake? That's how Esposito explained it."

In the end, Team Canada squeaked by with the Moscow series 4–3–1. Still, as one Canadian journalist put it, "We won the games; we lost a legend."

Around the turn of the century Russians developed a soccerlike game on ice with a cord-wound leather ball. Eleven men to a team played on a rink half the length of ice hockey's.

The Czechs introduced Canadian hockey to the Soviet Union in 1948. The government approved and, as usual, attached a heavy bankroll to a directive ordering development of the new sport. Moscow has played intensely but "comradely" games against Prague ever since.

In the spring of 1969, so as to smooth over some of the less than comradely tracks their tanks had left on the streets of the Czech capital the year before, the Soviet hockey squad was delivered to Prague as meek as a flock of sheep on its way to slaughter. Bombarded with rotten eggs, booed, cursed, slapped, and stomped, they stood under strict orders not to give in to "counterrevolutionary provocation." When the Czechs won, Party Secretary Gustav Husak had to call out troops to disperse the exultant demonstrators, who threatened to turn a hockey victory into another revolution. Every Czech game since has meant raw nerves and frustration for the Russians: they have license to clobber the Canadians and slam the Swedes as much as they please but have to suffer bloody noses and slashed foreheads from the Czechs as though they'd just been gently kissed.

Would Los Angeles Kings Dave "the Hammer" Schultz or Philadelphia Flyers André "Moose" Dupont ever be so cooperative with the Secretary of State in implementing U.S. foreign policy? For the Russians, there's no question. Their byword is discipline—the foundation of not only sports but the whole of Soviet society. Like any other people in the world, they find any excuse to avoid it. Unlike others, however, Russians seem also to need a strong boss who'll drive them hard at home for the sake of a muscular image abroad.

Stalin exterminated millions of Soviets. But even the generation that survived his rule is already beginning to miss the dead tyrant. "Stalin wouldn't get bogged down in all this bull with the Chinese," they mutter. "He'd order a preemptive strike at Peking and the whole damn thing would be done with."

After Israel's defeat of the Arabs in the Six-Day War, many Muscovites greeted each other ironically by covering their left eye in tribute to another strong man—Moshe Dayan. It was rumored that Dayan was actually a former colonel of the Soviet Army, his discipline and determination cultivated by the Moscow Academy of the General Staff.

Anatolii Tarasov's tight rein as a coach reflected Soviet life in microcosm: submission, flattery, and smiles to his face; envy, hatred, and denunciations behind his back. But Tarasov reacted to neither. Uniquely uncompromising, he permitted neither party higher-ups nor sports commissars to monkey with his strategies or meddle with his rosters. Eleven world championships and four Olympic gold medals had put him in a class by himself.

In twenty-five years of coaching, Tarasov trained several generations of athletes, many of whom have achieved acclaim throughout the world. Only Tarasov still dared tell them, "You're a star today, but come back past curfew tonight and you're shit tomorrow."

Every spring, like robins at a worm sale, Moscow boys in full gear line up for as much as two miles outside the Central Army Club sports complex. Inside, Tarasov and team members hold tryouts from the stands, watching the young knights in armor demonstrate skating skill and shooting power. After two days of soul-searching, Tarasov recruits fifty eleven- to fifteen-year-olds and disappears. Then, following his instructions to a T, the club's most experienced players work with the kids in their spare time, until those who survive the trials to age sixteen fall into Tarasov's hands once again. His criteria for promoting them include passing and stickhandling techniques—only if supported by endurance for endless training, sometimes around the clock.

Like their Canadian counterparts Don Murdoch and Dave Maloney, these youngsters have often grown up in poor working families from the suburbs to the sticks. They begin playing in never quite finished housing complexes, where in winter the gutted ground yields countless natural rinks to fence in for an alternative to high school: though they're bored with Tolstoi by Chapter 2 and doze off during tension-packed detective films, they never tire of lugging around forty pounds of protective equipment. Tarasov often assigns them a rink for around 1 A.M. They nap in the overbooked hall while waiting for their ice time and curl up again after the session (the Moscow subway closes down from one to six). When they get home, the rookies dump their equipment and hang sweaty jerseys across an already crowded single-room flat, where mother, father, and siblings scramble, stoop, and trip on their way out to work.

Quite early on the boys begin swigging the watery beer of the Soviet hinterlands, which they beef up with generous doses of vodka—even though they've seen Tarasov mercilessly expel some of his best players after detecting a trace of alcohol on their breath.

It's not every player that can stand Tarasov's grueling school: many leave for teams with an air of wine and song, such as the Wings or Spartak.

There are ten clubs in the Soviet major league. Of them, Central Army, the Dynamos, and Spartak are the most popular. The largest crowds are drawn by Spartak, which represents light industry and the city services; the poverty of the club, which can't even claim its own rink, has won the hearts of millions of Muscovites. Second is Dynamo, whose blue-and-white pennant stands for the police and security forces and attracts a mixed house. The Central Army Club, nineteen-time national champion, has the rinkside support of only a few strategically seated battalions, who utter not a sound unless authorized by their commanding officer.

Spartak Aleksandr Yakushev, lauded by Bobby Hull as the best left wing in the world, once admitted he'd never have made it in the Central Army Club; he wouldn't have stood for Tarasov's martial regime. A prolific scorer known for crossing the rink in a matter of seconds, the 6'3", 205-pound Yakushev has a kind of strength and determination that few NHL men can match. And he is fearless enough to admit his weaknesses—something one doesn't come across among other players, who seem to wear an armor of braggadocio as heavy as their protective gear.

Discussing the Buffalo Sabres game in 1975, Yakushev confessed, "From the moment the puck was dropped, I knew they were out to get me. Defenseman Jerry Korab held me, hooked me, cross-checked me into the boards. He was so obsessed with hunting me down, he never bothered playing the puck—real animal hockey. I was completely shook up; I couldn't calm down for the rest of the game."

In another interview Yakushev described how he felt during the '76 Innsbruck Olympics, which the Russians carried off: "We couldn't fall asleep the night before the final game. What was happening the next day is rare even once in a normal lifetime. Twice is still rarer; eight years is an enormous time in sports. You really have to get a good night's sleep. But there's no way. Your nerves are on edge. You think, the younger guys aren't sleeping—well, O.K., they're excited. But you've already been through an Olympiad. Where's your Olympic cool? I see Volodia Shchadrin lying there with his eyes open. Viktor Shalimov is tossing and turning. He wants to win so badly.

"Later, after we had been awarded the gold, Valerii Kharlamov told me, 'I was afraid even an empty net would be too much for me. For the first time in my life, I was afraid. No one was there. So how come I went up high with the shot? For an instant after the puck left my stick I thought it wouldn't go in. But I caught the net just under the crossbar.'

"Kharlamov's goal was our fourth. Mine was number three. I had been just as scared I'd miss; I'd never have forgiven myself. Later on everyone seemed to be shaking our hands. I made my way into the locker room, threw down my gloves, pulled up a bench, and had a drink of water. I couldn't get up. My fingers were trembling. I just sat there staring. Gena Tsygankov sat across from me, his jersey drenched with sweat and his face white as a sheet. God, were we wiped out!"

"And what about tomorrow?"

"Well, tomorrow—tomorrow's another game."

The popular Boris Maiorov, captain of the National Team for years, was of the temperamental type not infrequently described as a goon. A Dynamo alumnus but clearly lacking the don't-make-waves disposition of his colleagues in the police, Maiorov once described his teammates' superstitious foibles. The following is his recollection of the Grenoble Olympics, at which the Russians once again emerged victorious:

"I walked into a restaurant, met some of the Czechs, and started talking with Stanislav Kostka, their coach—although they say it's not a good idea to talk with your rivals before a game.

"I remember Stockholm in 1963: Coach Arkadii Chernyshëv noticed a coin lying tails up on the subway, which Russians consider a really good omen. He waited two extra stops, until no one was left on the train to notice, before picking it up. He stashed it in his pocket and carried it on him right up until the end of the championships. And we won. That reminds me: last year I found a shilling tails up in a Vienna hotel and kept it on me throughout the championships, too. Again we dumped them. There was no way I wasn't going to take that coin along to Grenoble."

Maiorov tells how one evening he noticed a woman on the team bus before setting out for a Czech game: "When Coach Chernyshëv got on I asked, 'Is she going with us?'

'Don't worry, Bob,' came the answer. 'I've already asked her to get off.' A woman on the bus is a really bad sign. We all remembered the time we lost three–four when some Russian tourist got on with his wife on our way to a Prague game in 1963.

"When the bus starts up, we also have a tradition of shouting at our interpreter, Sasha Urban, to tell us bedtime stories—you know, about the little animals in the forest."

Although that evening the woman got off the bus, the coins were carried, and the stories were told, the Russians lost anyway—leaving first place up to the outcome of the Czech-Swedish game two days later. Everyone on the Soviet team except goalie Viktor Konovalenko sat watching the game intently on TV in the hotel lobby. All Sweden had to do was tie it to give the Russians another shot at the gold. And halfway through the third period, they were leading 2–1. "Suddenly," says Maiorov, "Konovalenko shows up bleary-eyed in the lobby. Right away the Czechs even the score, two–two. There were thirteen minutes to go. 'Get the hell out of here,' we shouted. 'Everything was fine until you came in.' Konovalenko walked out again without a peep . . ."

Sweden rallied to a victory: Russia would play Canada for the gold that evening.

"On the bus," Maiorov goes on, "we all looked around to see whether there were any women hanging around. It was O.K. Then, in unison, we shouted at Urban: 'Tell us about the little critters!' Urban set about it dutifully, and everything went as usual."

The Russians became Olympic champions.

"After the game," Maiorov concludes his testimony, "a Moscow film director I know who was on vacation in Grenoble pushed his way past the guards into the locker

room. Earlier in the day he and another Russian had
missed their stop on their way to the Czechoslovakia-
Sweden game. When they finally took their seats by the
rink they felt chilly. They put up their collars and sat
neutrally silent through the whole game. As I said, it ended
in our favor. In the evening, heading for our game, they
missed the stop again—but this time on purpose. Again
they put up their collars, and again they sat silent throughout, even though they were dying to cheer for us out loud."

To keep the National Team training camp from turning
into a labor camp, the Sports Committee decided to split
up Tarasov's power by demoting him and appointing
Dynamos coach Arkadii Chernyshëv to the head position.
Chernyshëv is tall and thin, a bold, grandfatherly type who
affectionately shortens his players' first names to things
like Bosia, Venik, and Tolik. Tarasov, on the other hand,
barks out their last names like a sergeant at morning roll
call: "Comrade Firsov, why aren't you in place?" "Comrade Kharlamov, get off the field!" "Come on, Comrade
Tretiak, you think you can handle two plus two?"

Chernyshëv comes to workouts in a warm sweater and sits
in the stands sipping tea from a thermos. Tarasov skates
with his disciples in a peculiar woolen cap and complete
uniform, and holding a stick, the better to shoot at them
—verbally and physically. As leaders of the National Team,
the two former rivals called a détente: Tarasov needed
Chernyshëv's calm intelligence as a safety valve for his
own steam-boiler style.

In the sixties Tarasov put together a rough draft of his
theories in a line made up of Konstantin Loktev, Aleksandr Almetov, and Veniamin Aleksandrov. There was to
be no duplicating the others' assignment: like any good

Canadian line, they were to function as scorer, checker, and playmaker.

Loktev carried the puck well out in front. He played cat-and-mouse, constantly provoking his opponents into thinking he could be easily body-checked: since the puck was far away, he'd have no time to dodge or fake. Yet in fact he could jump aside fast enough to sweep right through the crease to an open corner. In addition, he could play it both ways—and, as a defenseman, deck any opponent or harass him so effectively that if the guy got into the Russian zone at all he'd be more dead than alive.

Almetov carried the puck in tight with his left hand, giving him a difficult-to-defend-against right-hand shot. He could follow a fake to the right with a behind-the-back pass to outsmart just about any defenseman.

Aleksandrov could fake left, fake right, and fake left again in a matter of seconds, making short shrift of his hopelessly confused opponent.

People used to say the line kept in touch by telepathy: each of them knew where his linemates were at every moment of the game. The line worked out a set play in which one of them would draw in the opposing defenders until another of his linemates was left alone in front of the goal.

It was while working with the Loktev-Almetov-Aleksandrov line that Tarasov made up his mind to base the Soviet offense on precision passing.

He broke this down into four points:

1. No defender can outskate a pass: a puck can hit 110 miles an hour, while few players can do more than 30.

2. Passing is more unexpected than stickhandling or faking.

3. Cross-ice passing is easy. Headmanning the puck to a

teammate far up ice is incomparably more difficult, but when executed with a quick flip of the wrist it triples the general pace and alters the whole quality of the game.

4. Passes should be directed not at the tip of the forward player's stick but slightly in front, counting on him to move into the free ice.

According to Tarasov, "Even if you're open—even if you can rush the puck yourself—keep moving it up ice by passing to a forward partner, *just because he's ahead.* And do it immediately. Immediately!" This makes it possible, he says, to keep the attack driving relentlessly forward and, to avoid icing, forces the players free of the puck to catch up to their partner skating ahead: every attacking player has to cross the blue line as quickly as possible. Storming the net in this way avoids tipping off the opposition, completely robbing it of the chance of anticipating your plans and organizing an effective defensive pattern.

In the late sixties, working with a line of Anatolii Firsov, Victor Polupanov, and Vladimir Vikulov, Tarasov refined his theory with the realization that a good defenseman can intercept even the most precise of passes if it doesn't carry an element of surprise.

He began experimenting with passes shot not off the blade's center but with a gentle flick of its toe—advancing the puck more accurately, eliminating the windup, and increasing unexpectedness. And the only way to master that kind of passing, he insisted, was for the players to quell their lust for excitement and infraction brinksmanship.

Anatolii Firsov, the Russian answer to Bobby Orr and probably the best Soviet player ever, never minded giving up the puck and never tried outplaying by flamboyant fakery. Sometimes he even intentionally lost control for a second, knowing he'd get the puck back soon enough. If his partners were covered, he split the defense and made skate-stick-skate passes to himself.

The line became adept at throwing the defense off guard by unexpectedly changing game tempo.

A typical up-ice rush by the line began with Firsov and Polupanov undertaking an unhurried latticework of passes in their own end. In the meantime Vikulov, playing off the puck, cruised toward the red line. The instant he was free, he'd immediately be hit with a long diagonal pass and dart out with the puck to the opponents' net.

Tarasov took every opportunity to promote camaraderie and teamwork among the linemates. For every international game, he had Firsov bring along a tape of his little daughter asking "Daddy and his buddies to give their all for our motherland." The players would listen with Russian tears in their eyes that said the child belonged to them all.

Other times, Tarasov would invite guests like cosmonauts Pavel Popovich or Georgii Berezhnoi to describe how frightened they had been to be alone in space but how they had conquered it. Half an hour later the squad would throw itself in front of an opponent's puck with no less courage than their predecessors blocking German bullets on the streets of Stalingrad.

Tarasov never tired of intoning his motto, "Unequivocal superiority over any hockey team in the world, NHL included."

Tarasov wasn't just shooting off at the mouth; he was only too happy to sacrifice his theories for the sake of adapting to change. He realized, for example, that the Canadians couldn't be overcome by great passing or lightning speed alone. If you want to pass, you've got to plough up an avenue for the puck. What do you do when NHL players—fine, technically, but also tough, mean, and self-sacrificing—gang up in the defensive end? You, too, need strength, staying power, and daring.

The Boris Mikhailov–Vladimir Petrov–Valerii Kharlamov line, which shook the Canadian legend in September 1972, was the culmination of Tarasov's work. He put them through a formidable conditioning program, the most difficult part of which was the off-ice land training: jumping, running, and deep knee bends with heavy weights; 30- and 100-meter sprints, sideways and backward sprints, sideways obstacle-course jumping jacks, relay races with a 20-pound dumbbell instead of a baton, one-on-one shoulder-carries in circles; somersaults, forward-roll series, leapfrog, 5-meter standing long jumps; boxing, sumo, and Greco-Roman wrestling; fireman's-carry basketball with a weighted ball; soccer and handball.

These were not the tedious exercises common to many training programs. They were fun, but forced the athletes to take on considerable physical loads at the same time.

For on-ice maneuvers, Tarasov established a point system. The following qualified: long diagonal passes; fakes; shots on net; picking up a loose puck from the goal, defensemen, or sideboards; forcing the opposition into a penalty.

Where an ordinary line chalked up 7 or 8 points per minute of play, the Mikhailov–Petrov–Kharlamov line logged 15 or 16. Earlier games now looked like slow motion.

Tarasov reasoned that his players' stance on the ice should differ from that of the Canadians.

The Canadians' stance is a function of their style of puck-handling, faking, and stick control: the body, bent slightly forward so the player can see both the puck and his nearest opponent, is tailored toward one-on-one play or battering-ram breakthroughs. The Russian's body, on the other hand, straightened up with shoulders back and head raised, gives him a wider field of vision and a better chance of getting his bearings. Since he can see several of his partners at once, it's easier to make a long pass.

For their hard-hitting style, the Canadians set their legs wide apart. The Russians keep their legs closer together, more comfortable for powerful thrusts and explosive sprints. In addition, when the point of support for push-off is closer to the gliding leg, it becomes possible to do quick cuts and figure-skating-like maneuvers.

It was the Mikhailov–Petrov–Kharlamov line that prompted Flyers defenseman Joe Watson to comment, "If you let the Russians skate around and play dipsy-doodle with the puck, they'll kill you . . ." Goalie Ken Dryden of the Montreal Canadiens admitted he once became so exasperated he screamed at the Russians, "Would you shoot already?"

They didn't. Instead they traced a monotonous network of long and short passes and faked slapshots to psych out the goalie. They seemed to be passing to open ice when in fact they were gaining a position for firing the puck into the goal—again keeping cool while burning up the opposition.

Just to be sure they stayed cool, Tarasov groomed the line to play chess in their spare time. It was a hit: Petrov and Mikhailov did nothing but play chess all day before the 1975 Rangers game. After twenty-three matches, the white queen disappeared. Perfectly cool, Petrov went out onto the rink, clobbered somebody over the head with his stick, apologized, and scored twice. After the game the coach handed him the queen in the locker room. Petrov put the pieces back on the board and coolly started in with game twenty-four then and there.

The Russians won the gold for the fourth time in a row at the Sapporo Olympics in February 1972. On arrival in Moscow, the players of the winning team are customarily called into a special Sports Committee bureau to be handed cash prizes according to their contribution to the victory. It might happen that Tretiak will pull in more than Petrov or that Kharlamov will outruble both his colleagues, but each is under strictest orders to keep the figure to himself. It is speculated that Olympic gold is valued at anywhere from $4,000 to $8,000, depending on the international prestige of the sport. In the case of hockey, the scales seem to be weighted toward the top.

A good Soviet hockey player's overall income, including bonuses, amounts to $15,000 per year—a far cry from the annual $60,000–$300,000 range of the Canadians, perhaps, yet a sum so huge for the average Russian that he finds himself at a loss as to how to spend it. Aleksandr Yakushev was being absolutely sincere when he told an American journalist he didn't understand why NHL players need such astronomical salaries. The figures that apply to American sports stars are in fact beyond the ken of any Russian, high- or low-paid, simply because there's nothing on which to spend the money in Soviet society and no idea of what's available abroad.

Aside from black marketeers and Georgian tycoons, who seem to be preoccupied with making millions for some vague idea of a rainy day, in the whole of the USSR there are only a handful of officially tolerated private estates: the royalties of writers Mikhail Sholokhov and Konstantin Simonov ($1 million plus); actor-singer-bandleader Leonid Utesov's garden-, pool-, and garage-equipped dacha ($200,000); the Fabergé collection of writer Maksim Gorky's family (about $100,000, plus dacha); or journalist Viktor Louis's veritable auto showroom, consisting of a Porsche 911, a Mercedes 240D, and a Landrover ($32,000, plus a two-story dacha with tennis courts).

The masses look upon these few as visitors from another planet. On the other hand, there's no worker who wouldn't welcome the slightest salary increase, if only as material recognition of his labor—unlike a mention in the papers or a cheap metal badge dangling from his chest.

In any event, when it comes to sports, coaches aren't ignored. Though they get their share of medals, titles, discount cars, and dachas, however, their cash prizes—even for Olympic gold—never exceed $1,500. So high was Tarasov's status, with every imaginable honor, that having more money was the only way he could still set himself apart from his colleagues. Taking advantage of the Sapporo Olympic victory, he decided no longer to lap up the little money doled out at the whim of the commission; he demanded that his prize match his players'. Senior Coach Chernyshёv, ever following the lead of his "junior" colleague, came along for the ride.

"Nyet," Chairman Pavlov replied firmly. Tarasov and Chernyshёv threatened to resign. The Sports Committee showed them where to sign the blanks on their pension forms. A popular Soviet hockey referee now living in Los Angeles told me: "Naturally, it was Tarasov's move we were amazed at, not the Sports Committee's. Remember, this is a society where no one's irreplaceable—where, if anyone wants to leave a job, he's sent packing with a bouquet of roses. Tarasov was a smart man, and he knew damn well no one was going to get down on his knees and beg him to stay. Only later, after talking with him privately, did I realize what he was banking on. He was certain that the world championships, which were to be held right after the Olympics, would be lost by the Soviets —which, by the way, they were. Then he was sure they'd ask him back."

They didn't—despite the defeat. Vsevolod Bobrov became senior coach.

Concurrently, in April 1972, the two-year-old talks between the Sports Committee and NHL chairman Clarence Campbell closed with a hard-and-fast agreement to hold the first world superseries that September between the all-stars of Team Canada and the Soviet Union. Ironically, in two years of dickering, Tarasov had been more instrumental than anyone else in bringing about the bargain. As early as 1969 he announced to Canadian sports writers who had been teasing him about the "invincible" Soviet amateurs: "I wouldn't care if we lost fifteen–zero. The score won't matter. What will is to see just how well our players stand up to the best pros in North America."

In truth Tarasov believed otherwise. After studying NHL game films for years, he was sure his men could at least give the pros a hard time. When asked what he thought about the games with Canada by Leonid Brezhnev, who may be even more concerned about hockey than soccer, Tarasov answered, "We'll play them on equal grounds. So what if we lose? We'll plead that the pros are *supposed* to be better."

But all of this was before February 1972. Once Tarasov resigned from the National Team his influence began rapidly deteriorating. Even his Army Club players became lazy over carrying out his orders, and Captain Boris Kulagin, his sour-faced, pill-popping deputy, reacted dyspeptically.

Then came the last straw. The Army Club was slaughtered by the Dynamos in the deciding game of the USSR championships, the Soviet version of a Stanley Cup playoff. When a referee seemed to have called a wrong puck, Tarasov ordered his team off the ice.

Defense Minister Marshal Andrei Grechko, who happened to be at the game, expressed displeasure at Colonel Tarasov's conduct; the next day the Sports Committee ordered that Tarasov be stripped of Honored Coach status and disqualified for two weeks. In turn, Tarasov resigned as senior coach of the Army Club. In May 1972 the post was assumed by Kulagin, who was instantly promoted to major. Tarasov left to work on a Ph.D. at the Moscow Institute of Physical Culture.

Two years passed. The Soviet hockey battleship alternately plowed the competitive waves and drifted unsteadily, as if barely steered by its new commanders.

One winter day in 1973 a citizen reeking of vodka collared now National Team coach Bobrov in an elevator of the Hotel Rossiia and demanded an explanation for the team's recent loss to Czechoslovakia. The coach wasn't exactly in the mood for a lecture. The man persisted, drawing a crowd on the twentieth floor while fingering the buttons of Bobrov's blazer. Finally the coach lost his patience, lifted his assailant off the floor, and pushed him out of the elevator—leaving some rather obvious signs of the fracas on his face in the process. The next day Bobrov was called into Granovskii Street: the citizen he had shoved out of the elevator turned out to be none other than the party secretary of one of the largest industrial regions of the USSR. Bobrov was invited to retire.

Kulagin's face began to acquire an uncharacteristic grin. Admitted on request to a hospital for stomach trouble, he was pronounced unsuited for the Army Club's rigidity. On his release he quickly found himself a position with the Moscow Wings and, with barely a pause, filled an abhorrent vacuum as senior coach of the National Team.

Meanwhile, Tarasov finished his thesis, and his old plot was suddenly played out after all: with Kulagin gone, he was asked to take over the ailing Army Club again and his titles were restored. Moscow readied itself for a miracle.

Nothing happened. The machine he had built for twenty-five years showed signs of coming apart after two years without him. Tretiak, Mikhailov, Petrov, and Kharlamov, the team's most influential nucleus, began conspiring to bite the hand that had fed them. After having it easy for a couple of years as pampered superstars under "Chuckles" Kulagin, they resented the return of Tarasov's screw-press program. On the other hand, they couldn't face him directly. The conspiracy involved training the way the coach wanted but blowing game after outrageous game.

Marshal Grechko was the first to catch wind of the problem. Even at seventy-two, the tall, powerful man played tennis before work every day at seven at the Army Club complex. One day, instead of heading for the General Staff at eight, he stopped by the hockey rink. He tried for hours to figure out what was going wrong with his most famous division. The intensive workouts, of course, showed nothing the matter.

Grechko commissioned an investigation. Every player

on the Central Army Club was called behind closed doors
and asked what was causing the trouble. And almost everyone gave the same answer: Tarasov. Many alluded to
Almetov, whose untimely death two years after retiring
from over a decade of Tarasovian training had been attributed to his radical change in life style.

Lieutenant Loktev became Army senior coach.

But that was not the end of Tarasov's career.

Two years ago Tarasov was invited by Brezhnev to take
over the Central Army soccer team. Tarasov's daughter,
figure-skating coach Tatiana, gave the following comment
about it: "He's so popular in his old age, he's done so
much for hockey, that he didn't need to take this on too.
I really don't think anyone else would have bothered or
dared. He's certainly not doing it for the glory: he just
can't not work. He runs at training sessions, although his
old legs are weak and his tendons torn. He can't just conduct the sessions with a mike: he has to torture himself.
He doesn't know how to live any other way."

In May 1977, for the first time in years, the Russians
finished third in the world hockey championships, after
Czechoslovakia and Sweden. And the reason was not so
much that they played badly as an absence of speed and
stamina.

Of all the posts in his checkered career, Tarasov now
holds only one: sports reporter for Tass. A long article
by him ran in newspapers across the country attributing
the slip to "the ignorance of coaches Boris Kulagin and
Konstantin Loktev," "the coaches' incompetence," "the
coaches' dull wits," "the coaches' confusion," "the coaches'
claptrap," and "the coaches' tactical illiteracy."

The old boy's attack didn't go unnoticed. Immediately

after the article appeared, Kulagin and Loktev were dismissed as coaches of the National Team and replaced by Tarasov's minion, Vladimir Tikhonov. Tarasov himself was appointed deputy chairman of the Soviet Hockey Federation.

Was it mere revenge that motivated the diatribe against his former colleague and pupil? Not at all. To Tarasov the essence of any job is unrelenting struggle—with oneself or others, whether compulsively pounding out a thesis at the typewriter or coaching a team at the rink. A championship team.

NINE

Hercules' Chemistry

The critical stress bursts upon a weight lifter in the two-hands clean-and-press when he boosts the barbell from his chest to the arms-fully-extended position. The weight crashes floorward, down his arms and onto his shoulders, his neck, his back and abdomen, and, finally, his legs, as if to break down the mountain of muscle he has evolved through years of training. He sucks in his breath and holds it; the air pressure quadruples in his lungs. His arteries contract and his blood pressure jumps. His heart and brain are cut off from a fresh supply of oxygenated blood. His face becomes a stage of distortion—an enactment of the gravity-defying drama. It is here that lifters have blacked out, collapsing under the bar onto the platform.

In an against-the-rules stab at saving their charges some of the strain, trainers schemed to facilitate the arms-only lift: barely discernible body shifts and jolts bouncing the weight up with the help of leg and trunk power.

Judges either failed to notice or chose not to, but protests began piling up at the Jury of Appeals and the number of off-platform interteam scuffles soared.

The clean-and-press became the bane of the sport, and in late 1972 the International Weightlifting Federation put an end to the problem by abolishing the lift in international competition. Of the traditional Olympic Three, only the snatch and the two-hands clean-and-jerk remained. This was as shocking as if sports potentates had replaced the 100-meter dash with 150. The technique and strategy of the contest had to be changed. No one had any idea of what to do about body weight; increasing weight had been the surest route to a successful press. The new rules affected Russians, however, for other reasons as well.

There has always been a cult of physical strength in Russia. The earliest folk heroes were lauded most for restraining wild horses, bending copper coins, and straightening iron horseshoes with their bare hands. In later centuries, crowds at carnivals fell into ecstasy when strongmen single-handedly lifted wagons or a horse's collar with five men hanging on. With the advent of the automobile, spectators were thrilled breathless when a giant got up unharmed after lying on the ground, having his belly covered with a wooden ramp and a truck run over him.

In the last twenty years the superheavyweight lifter has become a Russian trademark, his muscles drawing more respect from the average man than the most spectacular sputnik stuffed with every miracle of modern electronics. The more impressive the poundage the lifter works up into the air, of course, the higher the pedestal to which his country is elevated. The figures 500, 600, and 700 kilograms (this last soon to be taken)—the combined totals lifted from the press, snatch, and jerk—were imposing (translating to 1,100, 1,320, and 1,540 pounds, respectively): the zeros loomed victoriously like huge iron disks in the minds of the ever rapturous fans. Eliminating 200 kilograms' worth of press made the impressive arithmetic seem downright miserable. Worse yet, it looked like a diminution of the grandeur of Russia's mighty past, heroic present, and brilliant future.

"Mighty," "heroic," and "brilliant"—the words are apt today, but they could hardly have been applied to Soviet weight lifters of the forties and fifties, when American athletes dominated the world's competitive platforms. The names John Davis, Jim Bradford, Tommy Kono, and Norbert Shemansky were pronounced with awe by their Russian counterparts, who lagged far behind. Coach-philanthropist Bob Hoffman was declared a man to model after, his antisocialist affluence notwithstanding. American training manuals were translated, American strategies studied, bodybuilding researched, and competitions filmed.

And yet Russia, the Hercules of nations, trailed in producing Herculeses of its own. Paul Anderson's explosive records shattered Russian eardrums. When, in 1955, he visited the USSR, everyone who was anyone in the Moscow sports community came to his workout at the Dynamo gym. At 5'10", Anderson weighed in at 342 pounds, with three-foot-wide hips and nine-inch wrists. The minds of Moscow boggled.

Just for openers, he began with a new world-record press or two. Then, barefooted, he stepped up to 605 pounds on a chest-level stand.

"It's too risky," one of the Russian coaches whispered to Hoffman.

"Don't worry; he's done it back home, with a pair of safes hanging from an iron girder."

"Listen, I don't doubt he'll survive the weight. What I'm worried about is our made-in-Moscow barbell."

Anderson did ten squats with the weight, hoisted it back onto the stand, muttered "That's all!" in Russian, and walked into the locker room to a standing ovation.

The newspapers knew they'd have trouble reporting the foreign giant's feat to the public without insulting the Russian claim to physical prowess, so they decided to insult Anderson instead. The athlete was depicted as a one-of-a-kind genetic anomaly, a species other than human, a King Kong who'd be better off caged in a freak show.

Aleksei Medvedev, Soviet heavyweight champion at the time, wrote: "No matter how hard you work, you just can't get that kind of muscle by training alone. You've got to be born with it. Probably a lot of *real* athletes breathed easier when they heard he was moving to the pros. The American phenomenon could lead to such a spiraling of world records that we'd have to wait for another Paul Anderson to be born here before we could even think of beating them."

In time, though, the Russians broke into the 500 club the American had opened up and surpassed him both in bodyweight and barbell poundage. Now sports history could be rewritten. Anderson was proclaimed biologically all right, and his records the just reward of heavy training. Fifteen years later Medvedev apologized: "I'm sorry now that I once allowed myself to insult one of the greatest athletes of our age."

Air Force Lieutenant Yuri Vlasov was the first Russian to win the world championship. Tall, handsome, and nicely built, with light brown hair, deep-set gray eyes, and a classic profile, the Soviet flag-bearer at the Rome Olympics carried the pole at an unwavering right angle to his arm during his entire lap around the stadium. Wavering in his soul, however—contradictions tearing apart his heart and mind—made him a most atypical representative of Soviet youth.

The son of an early military adviser to Mao Tse-tung who had fallen victim to Stalin's purges, Vlasov began his education in the prestigious Suvorov Military School, its halls hung with the portraits of great generals. Required to study Napoleon's march on Moscow and bury himself in the battle of Berlin, he spent his time instead with Dostoevski's *Demons* and Gakkenshtadt's *The Path to Strength*— the latter banned because its author was a White Russian who had emigrated to London.

After graduating from the Air Force Academy, Vlasov found himself patrolling missile installments day and night amid the howling winds that swept across the hundreds of miles of desert around him. Only the words of Emile Verhaeren, "To delve so deep into oneself with dreams endurant/That pain, though real today, will dissipate like dust," kept the young officer from doing away with himself. As a beginning weight lifter he imagined life's coarseness concentrated in the multikilogram disks and resolved to subdue it by force of mind. The challenge was stimulating along the way, but once he had become Olympic champion and shattered all of Anderson's records with a 1,184¼-pound total, he lost interest in sports and decided to devote himself to writing.

Subduing the art of words turned out to be far harder than penetrating the mysteries of athletics. His sentences sprawled; the thoughts scattered, the flow stalled. Publishers expected stories about "positive heroes"; Vlasov gave them the charm of Italian girls, the tang of Chianti and Frascati, the warmth of Mediterranean beaches. The manuscripts kept coming back, and his prize money dwindled. He sold his car and took a coaching job at $140 a month.

Then, unexpectedly, he was chosen from among thousands of contenders to play Pierre Bezukhov in the screen version of *War and Peace*—a role that would have required the determined fighter in a sport of strength to portray the very personification of Tolstoian nonresistance. At the last minute, however, director Sergei Bondarchuk changed his mind and took the role for himself.

In all, Vlasov's life out of sports seemed a failure. He returned to the National Team to a comfortable $550-a-month stipend. The old challenge was over; now he was lifting weights to finance his dream of writing. And there was only one way to put away a bankroll big enough to last a few years: to capture the gold again at Tokyo.

Together with scientist Lev Matveev, Vlasov worked out a training schedule for an entire year in advance, a geometry in which the curves on his graph stood for gallons of sweat, scratches on his chest, bruises on his neck, skinned flesh from his palms. But the graph led to a plateau after which the wear and tear would vanish, the lungs would pull in more oxygen, the heart would pump more blood, the muscles would ripple with fresh tissue, and the weights would seem to lift themselves. It pointed to a time when once again no one in the world could keep him from the Olympic throne.

But reality interfered with his theory. A low-grade fever hovered over him month after month. The doctors inferred neuralgia.

Drenched with sweat, torpid with weakness, dazed with headaches, Vlasov's life was plagued by a nightmarish need for water. His body weight dropped sharply, and he couldn't bring himself to eat enough to compensate: salmon tasted like rags; steak, like rubber; kasha, like boiled sand. His writing became the only bright spot in a tunnel of torture. Every morning at nine, when Senior Coach Arkadii Vorobëv and the National Team set out for the gym, Vlasov stayed behind in his hotel room, took out some paper, and sat down at his desk to write.

He tried describing the grass, the woods, the river, the sun outside his window, everything that diverted him from torturous thoughts of the mocking kilograms. Paragraph after paragraph appeared sound until he reread them. His wastebasket filled to overflowing with crumpled sheets. He got up to empty it in the corridor.

Returning to his desk, his hand scribbled rapidly across the page; thickly covered sheets began accumulating on the table, not in the wastebasket. He had confronted his nemesis at last. Vlasov's study of his victory at the Rome Olympics follows:

A large hall, full of people, in front of me. A hush. I step up to the line. A record weight on the bar.

I adjust my trunks and support belt, sniff some bracer from the wad of cotton in my trainer's hand. I test the bar. Sleeve jams sometimes, won't turn. Hard on the wrists. Grip's perfect: the knurls cut into the palms. Worn down, but still sharp. Like emery, they strip skin off the chest and neck, exposing raw, red flesh. My wrists are locked. My hands won't lose it. My legs are apart, braced as solid as possible. Any more—any less—will be unstable: the bar won't go the way it should. I jiggle my feet for a stronger stance. I close my eyes and loosen up. My body hangs over the bar like a loose whip. I move my lips. Mumble my favorite verses. Ritual. It rouses me, helps get myself together.

"The blood of your fathers has turned to water in your

veins. Not your lot is it to be strong, as they were. Having tasted neither life's sorrow nor its joy, like a sickling you watch life through a glass. Your skin will shrivel, your muscles grow weak; tedium will devour your flesh, destroying desire; thought will congeal in your skull, and horror will stare at you from the mirror. Overcome yourself!"

"Overcome yourself!" I tremble. I seethe. I clench. I scan the hall. The reviewing stands, the people, the lights, slip past me.

I started wrong. To recover, to get the bar to my chest, I bent over too far.

I straighten up and concentrate on standing my ground, keeping my balance. If I budge my leg I'll lose the line of balance between the bar and my body. Even if they don't notice, it'll take its toll.

No: I stand firm, the bar on my chest. I gulp in the air and hold it. I'm still, muscles shackled. I let my chest take the weight, freeing my arms of some of it. They're weakened. My elbows are tight against my sides. I await the judge's clap, trembling. It's getting heavier.

I've leaned back too far! The bar's against my jugular: my head starts to buzz. If he holds out any longer, I'll never make it!

Clap!

I put everything into it. The bar seems to jump from my chest and drives upward. There's ringing in my ears. My muscles are humming with the strain, like bass strings—taut, thick catgut. I've got to get it past the sticking point. That's the worst. One muscle group switches off, transfers the strain to the next. Unprepared, it can't give me its best. The struggle could be over right here.

I drive myself. Like forcing myself, pressuring my power, into a narrow mold. I press.

I'm ready for a pitched battle; I expect it to resist. But the bar's slipped past the sticking point; something seems to be carrying it with my upstretched arms. I rivet it. It goes too far. The weight crashes down my back; I hear my spine snap. I'm losing my balance. I've got to keep standing!

A second more and my toes will shift: disqualification. I'm sure I've lost it. If only I'd kept my balance! I'm going to collapse, topple, like the walls of a gutted house!

People are shouting, urging me on. I'm not going to give up. I push back with my last ounce of strength. My body is all music. The bass strings, the most powerful muscles, thrum, rumble, and mingle with the interlacing wail of every tiny fibril. My feet are wriggling in my boots, but the boots stay immobilized. I can't lift them from the floor: against the rules.

I listen for the bar above my head. Everything in me focuses on it.

Hold on!

There's a sharp pain in my back, like I've been caned. I'm conscious of nothing but a flickering, mottled blur, the crowd noise coming from it. But I'm sustained by it. It keeps me from giving in to the pain, and my arms extend fully, lock into position.

Gkhyy! The air explodes from my lungs.

"Lift!" The judge.

The fatigue descends, envelops me like a huge sheet, heavy with moisture.

At 4 P.M., Vlasov gathered his manuscript together and left his room for the empty gym.

Leonid Zhabotinskii was a round-faced, lop-eared, red-haired ruffian, a street kid from Kharkov known for demonstrating his gentlemanly virtues by tossing the kids in rival gangs over the fence of the dance palace at the local park. At sixteen he stood 6' 2¾" and weighed a good 220 pounds.

"You're nothing but a bully and a slob," bawled the girl he fell in love with, summing up the facts in a nutshell. Zhabotinskii grabbed her, but changed his mind halfway to the fence. He returned her to the ground and swore he'd "get some culture."

In 1963 Zhabotinskii made a meteoric debut in weight lifting by breaking Norbert Shemansky's world record with a 165-kilogram two-hands snatch. The spectacle notwithstanding, Zhabotinskii wasn't given a thought as a serious contender to Vlasov. If nothing else, he had a reputation far and wide for being lazy as hell. Where Vlasov totaled 20 tons in the course of a training session, Zhabotinskii did only 5—and then he'd skip a week's workouts to make up for the effort. His managers would come to his room again and again for pep talks and interrogations. Zhaba ("Toad," in Russian) would lie silent in bed, looking vaguely agonized. Then, as soon as the bosses turned their backs to go, he'd give them the finger and jump out of bed for the nearest bar or billiard parlor.

Aleksei Medvedev, now a novice coach hunting for a disciple, decided to work on Zhabotinskii.

"I told him," Medvedev later wrote, "that a guy of his size and his already knockout success doesn't belong only to himself anymore. I told him he was beholden to the motherland, to the reputation of Soviet sports.

" 'Me?' He seemed genuinely startled. 'What about Vlasov?'

" 'All you have to do is set that goal for yourself, and you'll mow down even the great Vlasov.'

" 'Beat Vlasov . . .' He smiled, looking incredulous. He

was silent a moment. Then, suddenly: 'O.K. What do I have to do?'

" 'First of all, we have to set up a strict training schedule . . .'

"A mere month later Zhabotinskii told me:

" 'It looks like I'm going to make it to Tokyo.'

"I beamed with pleasure. He'd been grabbed by the impossible dream."

As had Medvedev himself, ever since Vlasov had ousted him from first place in 1958. Thanks to an absence of strong contenders, for ten years in a row Medvedev had found the Soviet championship a shoo-in, even with his mediocre results. But at international tournaments he never stood a chance. Nonetheless, his dream was of a world victory. At long last, when he had finally hit a 505-kilogram total—highest in the world after Anderson and the Argentine Humberto Selvetti—Medvedev was unceremoniously toppled by the mighty Vlasov and left behind without a future.

Medvedev quit sports for graduate school. He began researching Vlasov's training methods, observing his former rival day after day in the Central Army Club gym. After four years at it, he won his Ph.D.—a scrupulously detailed study of Vlasov's two-hands clean-and-jerk: approaching, adjusting his stance to find a strong base, testing the bar, finding the right grip, bending, splitting, shooting up with the weight to his chest, holding it there, and finally jerking it overhead and recovering his balance.

But Medvedev's study didn't stop there. Though he left it out of his report, he let nothing of the champion's personality escape his notice: his sentimentality, his vulnerability, his short temper—most of all, his openness, to the point of gullibility, with his rivals. And this information he shared, when the time came, with his student Zhabotinskii.

Six months before the Tokyo Olympics, the Sports Committee directed that the Soviet Union be represented by two men in the superheavyweights: Vlasov and Zhabotinskii. In the town of Dubny, where the National Team was training, the two athletes were isolated from lifters of less lofty weight categories, eating at a separate table and served by a special squad of waiters, who would hurry trays piled high with food to the ravenous pair.

Vlasov and Zhabotinskii sat facing each other day after day across breakfast, lunch, and dinner. Toad made short shrift of his food in a veritable sideshow of gastronomic impropriety: he stuffed his face with the salad, gulped down the milk, grabbed the meat with his hands, licked the grease from his fingers and the gravy from his chin, gnawed at the bread loaf, chomped every mouthful, sucked on the bones, gargled with his soup, paused to burp, dunked his face into the pudding, and finished by blowing his nose *à la Russe*—pressing one nostril closed and snorting the other out onto the floor. The meal over, he'd pat himself on the belly and belch at a decibel level that made the dishes rattle and the waiters cringe. To Vlasov, the anguish of weight lifting seemed like child's play compared to the ordeal of breaking bread with Toad.

When the champion went up to his room to write in peace and quiet, Toad hung his own door with a handwritten note reading DO NOT DISTURB: PREPARING FOR CONTEST and fell promptly asleep, snoring and farting, the walls and doors barely muffling his *Nachtmusik* of natural functions.

The moment Vlasov and his coach, Suren Bogdasarov, would show up in the gym, the crash of barbells in the opposite corner would announce the arrival of Zhabotin-skii and his trainer, Medvedev.

Bogdasarov had a marker attached to the champion's bar, so that when Vlasov raised the weight the device chalked the trajectory of the lift on a blackboard against an ideal curve. Toad demanded and got the identical mechanism.

A team of physicians attached electrodes to Vlasov's biceps to experiment with the effect the resultant rhythmic flexing would have on building his muscle size and strength. Zhabotinskii demanded his share of the scientific revolution and was supplied with a contingent of Vlasov's medical brigade. He quickly matched the 20 inches of Vlasov's arms, and his body weight shot past the champion's 275 to 352 pounds of his own.

The sessions began resembling a chase, revealing unexpectedly that the young contender had not only his own coach behind him but Senior Coach Vorobëv and the whole of the National Team as well.

Vlasov's intellectual, contemplative bent, as well as his apparent aloofness, was alien to the simple workers who made up the bulk of the team. His literary exercises, in which he immersed himself while the others were sweating away with exercises of their own at the gym, were taken as contempt for collectivism.

And there may have been some truth to their suspicion —not so much in terms of his dislike for individuals but in terms of his unwillingness to buy the ethic of Soviet collectivism with anything short of sober consideration. Under a verbal umbrella of friendship, equality, cooperation, and succor, the Soviet collective is more than anything an easily manipulable tool available to shrewd party functionaries for baiting, hounding, and coralling anyone they perceive as being out of step. The objects of this torment are usually especially intelligent or talented individuals, whose eminence or whose actual superiority threatens the stagnant gray equilibrium that is the foundation of Soviet society. When focused to attack, the collective turns into a glowering, dark, and terrible force, capable of ruining any person in any field. Sports is no exception.

Making Vlasov's life miserable wasn't easy, however, thanks to his proven service to the motherland and his public reputation. Still, if it wasn't possible to do it directly, the collective could always make the circumstances around him intolerable—slandering him behind his back, spreading rumors, ridiculing his fondness for literature. Under the pressure, Vlasov lit out for Moscow —providing exactly the excuse Vorobëv needed to send the Sports Committee a complaint about his willful capriciousness and egocentricity.

The situation got steadily worse. Vlasov refused to participate in the Soviet championships in Kiev—considered a general run-through for Tokyo—and Zhabotinskii was named champion. The newspapers began spreading it about that Vlasov was chickenhearted to begin with and had very simply gotten a case of cold feet.

Meanwhile, training at home again in Moscow's Central Army Club gym against graphs and curves alone, Vlasov finally reached his threshold and sailed over like a runner with a second wind. His muscles tingled with freshness. Fatigue and listlessness turned into acuity of movement. At an international tournament in Podolsk a month before the Olympics, he broke three world marks, lifting a fantastic total of 580 kilograms.

That night, for the first time in his life, Zhabotinskii was troubled by insomnia—tossing and turning, repeating over and over, "What a weight!" The next morning, with a deep sigh, he asked his coach what to do.

"Win," answered Medvedev, now silently more than unsure in his reliance on a strategy based on theories of Vlasov's weakness of character.

Tokyo, October 18, 1964: Vlasov is leading Zhabotinskii by 5 kilograms and two fresh world records in the press and the clean-and-jerk. No one doubts he'll win it: not the judges, nor the press, nor the public—nor Vlasov himself.

Zhabotinskii orders 200 kilograms for his first attempt in the snatch. The relatively low weight for the lagging contender can only mean that Toad is willing to live with the imminent defeat. Panicked, his narrowed eyes propping his strip of forehead, he somehow pulls it off.

In the warm-up room, he goes up to Vlasov: "Let's call it off, Yura. I've had it with competing. The gold is obviously yours. Why wreck ourselves on another couple of attempts?"

Vlasov won't agree. This day is his last in the sport, his farewell to iron. He pictures a table with sharpened pencils and reams of clean white paper, materials without which he can no longer imagine his life and for the sake of which he's in the fight even now. He wants a memorable exit: with the gold medal and with world records in every class of the set. He asks for 210. The lift is clean, easy, continuous.

Zhabotinskii jumps to 217.5. What's going on? Is he showing off? Is he bluffing? But it's his only chance to catch up with the champion. He tries it, pulls the bar just above knee level, and lets it drop with a clang. With a disappointed sweep of the hand he walks out. He looks broken, destroyed by the struggle. He smiles weakly, hugs his rival, congratulates him on winning first place, musters a few animated words about the victory of the Soviet team being what counts most, whoever brings home the gold.

Now it's Vlasov's last attempt. Relaxedly he examines his sturdy black leather boots. He rubs the soles fastidiously with rosin so as not to slip. The names of the rivals he's done in are painted in red across the tops: Medvedev, Anderson, Bradford, Shemansky, Ashman . . . He'll add Zhabotinskii to the list today and retire his shoes in his private hall of fame.

All he needs for the gold is 215. Even 212.5. But for his farewell finale he wants to hear the sound of another record: 217.5.

The weight travels up smoothly, of a piece with his body, like a rocket casting off a stage every fraction of a second. He's extended evenly, it's over his head, but he can't fix it there. It shakes. He tries to catch his balance, steps forward. He can't get the stability he needs. He moves across the platform, dancing after the weight, trying to catch the center of gravity. A second more and either bad balance or the load itself will send him into a spin, crashing to the platform.

Memory dutifully retrieves a six-year-old image: chasing after a barbell, he had chipped his vertebrae. The crunch and the searing pain of the torn ligaments had muffled the roar of the crowd and turned the yellow lights to blood-red.

The flashback has done its trick. Vlasov hurls down the weight, satisfied just to be champion. The glory of three records running can't warrant the risk.

Now Zhabotinskii gets up on the platform, winks at

Medvedev, and fixes the 217.5 without a hitch. Winner and new Olympic champion.

Vlasov fully realizes his defeat only when he sees the crowd of journalists around him suddenly break up and cluster densely around Zhabotinskii in the opposite corner. Embarrassedly he adjusts his glasses, not knowing where to go, still failing to understand how Toad, broken down by competition half an hour before, sure of Vlasov's victory, could have done it: with what miraculous burst of strength?

Late that night in his hotel, Vlasov summons a picture of the duel and realizes he's been duped, gulled like a schoolboy, by the most elementary of psychological tactics.

"I was choked with tears," he wrote ten years later. "I flung the silver medal through the window. Damned, miserable mockery of an award! Was that it, the return for all the years of frenzied study, self-mastery, struggle, unyielding self-sacrifice? A silver disk on a colored ribbon? Inwardly I renounced the trophy, wanted nothing to do with it. I had always revered the purity, the impartiality of contests of strength. That night I understood that there is a kind of strength that has nothing to do with justice."

In the four years between Tokyo and Mexico City, Zhabotinskii reaped a Soviet champion's harvest.

He was promoted from simple soldier to senior lieutenant. He moved to Zaporozhe, where he was given a glass-and-steel house overlooking the Dnieper. He was appointed director of the local sports palace (once he came to the office, sat on the desk, and it collapsed beneath his weight; he never appeared again, ordering his salary mailed to his home), lecturer at the local teachers' college (when students asked for information on the Tokyo Olympics,

he'd give them the dope on the city's better whorehouses),
and a member of the municipal party committee (not in
recognition of his political merits, but to justify packing
his four refrigerators with quality foods available only in
stores reserved for public officials).

"I wanna have my own gym!" the heavyweight king now
raged, and ground was broken for a foundation. Once the
floor had been laid, he changed his mind. A flame flared
in his soul for greater sophistication in his surroundings.

He moved to Kiev, the capital of the Ukraine and considered the most appealing city of the country after Moscow
and Leningrad. But dozens of other champions had had
the same idea. He was shown less attention, and his benefits
were now shared with the rest. He returned to Zaporozhe
and swore to the local commissar he'd stay there till the
end of his days. He got a dacha.

Toad became preoccupied with perpetuating his crown
into eternity. Deeply convinced he could preserve his
strength forever by economizing on energy, he refused to
push himself at workouts and missed more than a few
tournaments.

At Mexico his principle came off swimmingly. With a
1,262-pound total—not advancing the Tokyo statistic by
so much as a gram—he won the gold again. After a first-
attempt snatch of 202 (15.5 kilograms less than Tokyo),
confident that American Joe Dube and Belgian Serge
Reding couldn't touch him, Toad declined the next two
attempts. The crowd booed and stamped, demanding that
the champion go on with his muscle show. Toad guffawed
in the warm-up room, gave the audience the beloved
finger, and kept repeating, "Lifting a barbell ain't like
eating no watermelon."

The next morning he propped himself against the fence

of the Olympic Village and began dealing in his own brand of international relations: exchanging badges, souvenir pins, and medals.

French cameramen asked him to hoist their own hero— the coxswain of the French eight-man sculls.

"I can't do it," said the champion.

"He only weighs ninety pounds!"

"It's wasting my energy."

One of the cameramen flashed a shiny badge. Toad opened up negotiations. When he had pocketed three more of the French badges, the show at last got under way.

The Soviet screenwriter Vasilii Chichkov, in town for a documentary on the Olympics, approached timidly. Chichkov's screenplay had Toad going to Plaza Garibaldi to be greeted "spontaneously" by a mariachi band. A press badge glistened on his jacket. Toad fingered it.

"Trade?"

"Sorry."

"Then I'm not going to the shooting."

Much cajoling later, he agreed, having found out that the blond, blue-eyed Olympic gymnastics champion Natasha Kuchinskaia would be going along.

"I'm gonna go change," Toad mumbled, and lumbered away like a sleepy bear.

Half an hour passed. Chichkov went upstairs to check. Zhabotinskii was lying in bed, the same pants and boots still on.

"C'mon, Leonid, we're all waiting!"

"I can't. When I was putting on my shirt I got dizzy. I figured, why should I?"

Chichkov complained to Sports Committee chairman Sergei Pavlov. He returned the next morning to the Village, flanked by a couple of cameramen.

Toad was occupying the same spot by the fence, trading excitedly, both hands cupping badges, his sombrero weighted down by metal trinkets from all over the world and flopping over his head.

"How do you feel, Leonid?"

"How do you think? Sick, thanks to you and your complaint to Pavlov."

Chichkov patiently explained what enormous social value a film would have where millions of moviegoers could see their great heavyweight idol in action, and what inspiration they'd derive from it.

"Anyway, Natasha's not here anymore," Toad persisted. More haggling ensued.

In the end, a pair of cars headed toward Plaza Garibaldi. Waiting for a red light on Avenida Insurgentes, Zhabotinskii was recognized by a driver in the next lane, who jumped out of his vehicle, demanded an autograph, rushed back to the wheel, and began honking incessantly—apparently a Mexican signal that some superstar is riding down the street. Within minutes all eight lanes of traffic joined in the noisemaking. Passers-by turned around and started chasing after the cavalcade.

At the next light, cars in every lane began disgorging riders, who started pounding their hoods and fenders and yelling "*Viva* Zhabotinskii!" By the time the cavalcade had driven up to the plaza, hundreds more had taken up the chant.

Toad emerged from his car like a monument come alive. The mob started grabbing his hands, jumping onto his back, snatching at his sombrero, mussing his hair, and climbing onto his shoulders. Toad roared "Fuck you!" through the melee to Chichkov and his cameramen, who were delightedly filming the scene from a comfortable distance. Then he bulldozed himself back into the car, burst in, slammed the door, and locked it behind him.

"Hold it a minute!" shouted the celebrity-starved Latins, who began barricading the car.

Two mariachis with guitars clambered onto the roof, which they appeared to take for a dance floor, and began swaying to a chorus of "Mexico-rah, rah, rah!" The crowd jacked up the rear bumper. Chichkov turned on the ignition and rammed the stick into first. Nothing.

The moment had finally come: Toad knew it was time to put out a little of his long-pent-up energy. He jumped out of the car, dragged the mariachis off the roof, and boosted them into the air like a pair of dumbbells. His face left no shadow of a doubt that their landing would be anything but soft. The fracas was over.

When he got home, the first thing Toad did was to check his pockets. His wallet, with all his papers and money, had vanished.

Chichkov returned to Plaza Garibaldi. A policeman heard him out patiently.

"You mean Zhabotinskii—the strongest man in the world?"

"Right."

"His wallet's gone?"

"Exactly."

"That's some souvenir, Señor."

In 1965 Zhabotinskii was jolted by a stabbing pain in his lower back while swimming in the Black Sea. The giant was rushed to the hospital writhing and moaning. Urinalysis and an X-ray of his kidneys showed nothing, and in two hours the pain had subsided.

A year passed, and a second, and a third, and the condition never once reappeared. But Zhabotinskii wasn't satisfied. He was sure something had to be wrong in his huge body, which labored constantly under the pressure of tremendous weights. He threatened his doctors, demanding that they give him a clear-cut diagnosis of an incident that had come and gone three years before.

"At least give me pills for the pain if it ever happens again," he wheedled. They supplied him with tranquilizers.

But the expectation of trouble obsessed him. At home in Zaporozhe or at the Dubny training camp, Toad met each sunrise with a urine sample. At first he used small plastic cups. Then he switched to larger bottles. Finally he issued a memo that his urine be scrutinized, nonstop, twenty-four hours a day. A two-gallon jug was dug up and an assistant was charged exclusively with holding it nearby throughout his daily routine. But Toad entrusted no one with the delivery of the liquid to the lab. It became his morning exercise to jog through the streets in his warm-up suit, shopping bag in hand, disguising the precious cargo. Inside the clinic, jostling other clients in line with pettier samples, the champion bypassed the regular admissions window altogether, it being too small for his container. Doors marked NO ENTRANCE were opened wide for him, and every nurse available was switched from regular duty to handling and processing the urine sample of the VIP. Every test was negative.

Zhabotinskii would have no truck with the analysis. One day he'd lie in bed frustrated and depressed, and the next, storm into the gym midway through a workout and instigate general hysteria.

In 1969, a Lenfilm movie crew came to shoot him in action at Dubny. When the cameras had been set up and the motors had already begun to hum, Toad hurled down his barbell, grabbed an Arriflex and tripod together, and smashed them against a wall.

"Get out of here!" he shouted. "Get the hell out of here!" He motioned over to new National Team senior coach Artur Antson (Vorobëv having retired and Zhabotinskii having replaced Medvedev with Efim Aizenshtadt, who wasn't so much his coach as his valet and porter) and demanded to know who had let "the movie schmucks" in in the first place without his personal approval. Antson apologized, and the Leningraders too—having no idea what for, since the Sports Committee had granted its sanction and Toad had been informed of it long in advance.

That evening Zhabotinskii had a change of heart. His face a mixture of good will and sadness, he trudged over to the filmmakers' hotel followed by his assistants, laden with cakes, brandies, and fruits. Putting his elephantine arm around the shoulder of cameraman Evgenii Shlugeit, a guitarist and singer, he sighed, "Play me something for the soul, son." Shlugeit was thirty-three at the time; Zhabotinskii, thirty-one.

In the 1969 world championships in Warsaw, Zhabotinskii gave up the gold to Dube without even seeing the competition to the end. His obsession with pain had become more than he could manage, and for the first time he found himself unable to say whether the whole thing had been real or imagined. But a morbid fantasy had gotten the better of him: the premonition he'd expire right on the platform, in the middle of a snatch. He literally went running from the stage and out of Warsaw.

For a year and a half he secluded himself, not training, eaten by doubt, searching for physical ills. Finally, in 1971, the Kiev physician Boris Goikhman found a small kidney stone after dozens of X-rays. Had it been hidden so deeply for six years since his Black Sea attack? Or had it accumulated by the mental strain, the fantastic pressure Zhabotinskii had wrought upon himself? Any possible answer lay buried under the hail of accusations among the multitude of physicians who had kept an eye on him along the way. The surgery to remove the stone was without complication and turned him into a new man. With youthful vigor, Toad dove into the battle once again. But it was too late. Every one of his world records had been broken. Vasilii Alekseev's star had begun to glitter on the weight-lifting horizon.

Alekseev took third place at the 1969 Soviet championship, but he scratched "I want to be first" across a photo of the prizewinners. "Next year I'm going to *press* the weight Toad snatched today," he declared to the sports officials.

"Chutzpah," croaked Toad, who had snatched 210 kilograms.

In January 1970 Alekseev not only pressed 219.5 but beat the world-record total in the bargain with 595.

A month later a squabble arose over whom the new Hercules owed his achievements to and whether he was deserving at all of the name of Soviet champion in light of his periodic slaps in the face of the collective he had trained with.

On February 24 a letter signed by Olympic champion Aleksei Vakhonin appeared in *Komsomolskaia Pravda*:

> Alekseev has the gall to attribute his success to Moscow Trud's trainer Aleksandr Chuzhin alone, and Chuzhin has the temerity to affirm it in interviews! The truth is that

when Comrade Alekseev first showed up in the city of Shakhty, in 1966, and applied to Rudolf Pliukfelder's school, it was our collective that helped him find an apartment and a job. Our heavyweight isn't exactly easy to get along with. This was particularly obvious when Comrade Alekseev got stronger and began building some confidence on the platform. The collective criticized him several times for lacking self-control. More than a couple of pretty bitter conflicts were sparked last summer alone.

Alekseev should have acknowledged his comrades' honest criticism, like everybody else, and been done with it.

Not Alekseev. He blew up at Pliukfelder and called Chuzhin his trainer just to retaliate. So Comrade Alekseev has flown from our nest. But don't think that's left us impoverished—we'll have many more world-class athletes before we're through.

And just one more thing: can it never have occurred to Chuzhin that the laurels he's now wearing are stolen from someone else's head?

The times changed, but the tune remained the same. Tokyo middleweight champion Pliukfelder had built a stable of weight lifters under the auspices of the wealthy Yuzhnaia mine and had had miners flown in from all over the country. He propelled Vladimir Kurentsov to Olympic gold over the "Iron Hawaiian," Tommy Kono, as well as Aleksei Vakhonin and Dave Rigert.

An ethnic German, tough-minded and pedantic, Pliukfelder brooked no deviation in his stable from his methods of champion-breeding. This, however, failed to coincide with Alekseev's ironclad obstinacy. The "gold miners" joined forces to attack the rebel through the tried and true collective boot in the rear.

Komsomolskaia Pravda, still betting on the faltering but not yet outcrowned Zhabotinskii and considering Alekseev too wet behind the ears to take the throne himself, had been willing to risk publishing Vakhonin's letter: another in its catalogue of crusades against declining moral standards.

The next month, at an international tournament in Podolsk, Alekseev burst open the 600 club and solemnly dedicated every kilogram of it to the hundredth anniversary of Lenin's birth. The Central Committee of the Young Communist League ordered *Komsomolskaia Pravda* to reverse itself and recommended the new hero for red-carpet treatment. The front page of the paper carried the news in block letters: MARCH 19, 1970: A NEW ERA IN WEIGHT-LIFTING HISTORY BEGAN TODAY AT 21:31 HOURS: THE COSMIC BARRIER OF 600 HAS BEEN BROKEN BY A SOVIET ATHLETE.

From that moment on, Alekseev felt free to declare the Shakhty collective "a bunch of shit-eaters and ass-lickers." This time his critics held their collective tongue.

A veritable alchemist on his march through the European, world, and Olympic competitions, turning every bar he touched to gold, he expanded his living space from a one-room apartment to a two-bedroom house with a garage, a game and billiards room, a weight-lifting room, a garden, and a vineyard—all behind a fence and guarded by a growling dog, so that foes passing by and overhearing Tom Jones on his stereo had no alternative but to mutter in impotent envy, "Damned capitalist!"

The media presented Alekseev's occupation as logger, miner, student, engineer, phys. ed. instructor, and chemical-factory foreman all at once—the "jobs" being the sources merely of monetary donations, with the "employers" fighting like cats and dogs for recognition as his sponsor.

After two years on the throne, Alekseev fired Chuzhin, proclaiming that all he had to do was listen to his own body's signals and there'd be no better coach for him in the world.

With a few dozen world records to his name, Alekseev was asked why he was pushing so hard. His answer was unevasive: "To keep my rivals so far behind in the dust that they wouldn't even dream of beating me."

Well, maybe so. But there was another answer he had prudently omitted: money. By Soviet regulation, every world record swept up by one of its loyal sons and daughters is greeted with a prize. Before Alekseev's time this came to a neat $1,500 per. But on June 27, 1971, having shattered seven world marks in a single evening in Moscow's Gorky Park, Alekseev forced the Ministry of Finance to reevaluate. A roadblock was raised to stave off the unforeseen drain on the national treasury: a record would bring money only if established at international competitions. A trifle: in the following two years, Alekseev blessed the motherland by slashing the record ten times more.

Deeply troubled, the Soviet economists reduced the prize to $700. Alekseev retaliated with twenty-six blows in a row to the state pocketbook.

Trapped, the Ministry of Finance was all but ready to read the *Wall Street Journal* to stop the raging power-broker. By 1976, Alekseev had totaled eighty world records, upon which he took a socialist pledge to double the figure in honor of the Moscow Games in 1980.

On retiring from Sports in 1964, Vlasov's comment about Zhabotinskii was, "I just can't compete with a pig." Ten years later, the two athletes met again, this time at Vlasov's apartment. Zhabotinskii's thundering bass boomed through the two small rooms. He paced nervously from corner to corner and finally sat himself down in an armchair, which all but disappeared under his still-colossal bulk. After his surgery, Zhabotinskii had picked up one more world record in the clean and jerk, but it seemed as easily lost as a frail sapling forgotten in Alekseev's triumphal forest.

Though strapping and potent as ever, now that he was liberated from his *maladie sans maladie* Toad was no longer needed by the National Team, nor was he up to snuff for international tournaments. He blamed his rejection on official hypocrisy and accused his competitors of groveling. And he spoke of the sting of sudden solitude.

Feelings like these were no more than a memory for Vlasov, who had by that time published two books and edited a best-selling opus based on his father's diaries. He was in demand for interviews by newspapers and for personal appearances by television and movie studios. And he was recognized at last as an author. Nor had he become a hack, replacing recriminations with sugar-coated prose to please the party censors. Still, he had mastered the Soviet art of survival, the craft of maneuvering to secure himself a reasonably honest but comfortable life. He started painting his sports days in softer hues.

"Sitting there with Zhabotinskii," he wrote, "my weight-lifting years took on new meaning. The struggle now seemed straightforward, free of hypocrisy, noble and worthwhile. I felt none of the animosity toward Zhabotinskii I'd expected. Rather, I empathized, I understood him. As I listened to him I found myself wishing him luck.

"Why? I used to be out there with him. I felt as though there was a part of myself in him, a piece of my past. He was my comrade, after all; he worked his way to the top with the same grueling workouts, the same torturous trials, as I. When he was knocked down, he pulled himself back up, and when they'd given up on him, he gave them a new record for his weight-class.

"But how those trials had changed him! It was he and it wasn't. I had remembered him so differently!

" 'Don't you resent Tokyo?' he asked me suddenly. 'But what can you do? You've got to work, fight for first place, the gold medal.'

"I was taken aback, and I muttered something or other.

" 'I'm glad for you,' he added. 'Your latest book is really something fine.' "

Asked about his predecessors, Vasilii Alekseev commented first on Vlasov: "Yuri Vlasov was enormously hardworking, but he underestimated the value of technique and failed to make the most of his potential. Leonid Zhabotinskii was exactly the opposite. Even though he was heavier, he had much less staying power. On the other hand, he had a feeling for barbells, an unusually fine rapport with the apparatus. My advantage over both of them is that I know exactly where I'm going, I have a will to win, and I have an ability to keep up an incomparably more intensive training program."

Yuri Vlasov usually refuses to discuss Alekseev and even avoids mentioning the name of the current king. But his comments about Soviet sports in general are more than pointed: "Frankly, I don't know everything that goes on in Soviet sports, nor do I like all of what I do know. For example, I don't have much to say for athletes who gain weight endlessly in the pursuit of new lifting records. It's true they can build some strength that way, but that sort of bulk is abnormal, ugly. They're choked with flesh and short of breath, the slaves of their bellies. And that has nothing whatever in common with real strength, with the harmonious development of the man that sports is supposed to be all about."

July 27, 1976: the Olympic competition at St. Michel Arena, Montreal. Alekseev, the star Soviet Hercules, lays his 344 pounds on a wooden table in the warm-up room. A pair of masseurs dance an energetic mixture of the Charleston and the hustle on his back. The more violently they kick him, the broader becomes his smile, the lower the cameramen stoop to snap his expression. Grunting and tossing the masseurs from his back like a dump truck, he gets up and begins an inspection tour of the other contestants, busy with their barbells. He halts and looks intently at the barrel-like East German, Gerd Bonk, his only potential rival, as if to psych him out. But he's no more than posing for the cameramen, who ask him to make a few more passes, winking and grinning.

Back on the table, with massage oils poured over his shoulders, four hands drum along the small of his back. The faces of the masseurs are sweatier than that of the champion, who occasionally takes a sip of black coffee.

Out by the platform, two other assistants hustle on and off, computing the scores and calculating the time remaining until Alekseev's first attempt. They begin barking in Russian and shepherd away the cameramen.

Alekseev smiles slyly and winks over at the filmmakers. He walks onto the platform, dusts his hands with talc, spits on his palms, and moves lazily toward the bar, looking at it haughtily, even contemptuously. He adjusts the leather support belt beneath his royal belly and drops his hands relaxedly to his sides. His muscles flow soft and elastic along his arms, unlike the useless bulge and definition characteristic of body-builders.

He snatches the huge weight in a single, even, organic motion, raising the barbell over his head as if it were a woolen sweater. (Some athletes approach the weight with closed eyes, hands forward as though feeling their way in the dark; others steal up to it like a cinema sleuth after a wary target; still others run up to it headlong, with guttural cries, kicking it forcefully. They blink, pace, mutter, blush, pray, cross themselves, or raise their hands imploringly skyward. Lifting the weights, others bellow like wounded buffaloes. If the lift is good, they hurl their massive bodies to the floor, kissing the iron. If no good, they moan, they gasp frighteningly, they beat themselves over the head.)

Alekseev waddles off the platform like any Russian *muzhik* after a day's work well done—he might as easily have been felling trees, mining coal, or laying bricks. Today he happens to be lifting weights, but tomorrow, if asked nicely, he'll be eager to tow an ailing tractor. Back in the warm-up room, he sits down on a hard cot and starts bending over to untie his shoes, but his monstrous paunch gets in his way. The blood rushes to his face, turning it a deep purple-red. He begins puffing heavily, and beads of sweat form on his forehead, nose, and chin. He leans back, shoes still laced.

"Hey!" he grunts in an imperious tone that covers his dismay.

A moment later the king's assistants are kneeling at his feet.

About the Author

YURI BROKHIN graduated from the Moscow Institute of Cinematography and worked as scriptwriter and director for Soviet television and film. In 1973 he came to the United States and became a full-time lecturer at the State University of New York at Albany. He is a contributor to the *New York Times Magazine* as well as magazines all over the world, and has directed and written over thirty films, including *The Days of Doctor Berezov,* which won an Honorary Prize at the 8th International Film Festival in Cracow, Poland. His first book, *Hustling on Gorky Street,* was published in 1975.

Mr. Brokhin, a U.S. Permanent Resident, currently lives in New York City.